Overworked and Undervalued

Overworked and Undervalued

Black Women and Success in America

*Edited by Rosalyn D. Davis
and Sharon L. Bowman*

LEXINGTON BOOKS
Lanham • Boulder • New York • London

Published by Lexington Books
An imprint of The Rowman & Littlefield Publishing Group, Inc.
4501 Forbes Boulevard, Suite 200, Lanham, Maryland 20706
www.rowman.com

86-90 Paul Street, London EC2A 4NE

Copyright © 2023 by The Rowman & Littlefield Publishing Group, Inc.

All rights reserved. No part of this book may be reproduced in any form or by any electronic or mechanical means, including information storage and retrieval systems, without written permission from the publisher, except by a reviewer who may quote passages in a review.

British Library Cataloguing in Publication Information Available

Library of Congress Cataloging-in-Publication Data

Names: Davis, Rosalyn D., editor. | Bowman, Sharon L., editor.
Title: Overworked and undervalued : black women and success in America / edited by Rosalyn D. Davis and Sharon L. Bowman.
Description: Lanham : Lexington Books, [2023] | Includes bibliographical references and index.
Identifiers: LCCN 2022040535 (print) | LCCN 2022040536 (ebook) | ISBN 9781666907742 (cloth) | ISBN 9781666907766 (paper) | ISBN 9781666907759 (ebook)
Subjects: LCSH: Success—Psychological aspects. | Black people—Race identity. | African American women—Psychology.
Classification: LCC BF637.S8 O898 2023 (print) | LCC BF637.S8 (ebook) | DDC 158.1089/96073—dc23/eng/20221021
LC record available at https://lccn.loc.gov/2022040535
LC ebook record available at https://lccn.loc.gov/2022040536

This book is dedicated to the women who helped us become who we are: family, teachers, role models, and mentors. Without them, we could not have survived. It is also dedicated to Black women whose power has not been contained: Michelle Obama, Kamala Harris, Serena and Venus Williams, Simone Biles, Diane Nash, Ketanji Brown Jackson, Stacey Abrams, Keisha Lance Bottoms, and countless others who we know have been overworked, and likely felt undervalued, in their careers. We value you. We love you. We hope we represented you well and made you proud.

Contents

Overworked and Undervalued: An Introduction   ix
Rosalyn D. Davis and Sharon L. Bowman

Chapter 1: Shine Brightly, Diamonds   1
Kimberly Morris

Chapter 2: For the Black Girls with Difficult Names and Big Personalities, You Are Seen and Loved   17
Rosalyn D. Davis

Chapter 3: We Don't Owe You a Smile   31
Jovan Shumpert

Chapter 4: Find Your Replacements   43
Rosalyn D. Davis and Shantel Gaillard

Chapter 5: I Need No Qualifiers   55
Vanessa Costello-Harris

Chapter 6: This Is America   83
Rosalyn D. Davis

Chapter 7: Black Girl Magic Is Not Going to Kill Us   95
Rana Dotson and Rosalyn D. Davis

Chapter 8: Please Tell Us How to Fix the Problem of the Problematic Women of Color   109
Rosalyn D. Davis

Chapter 9: Random Reflections at 3 A.M.   121
Sharon L. Bowman

Conclusion: Overworked and Undervalued, a Culmination 133
Rosalyn D. Davis and Sharon L. Bowman

Index 139

About the Contributors 143

Overworked and Undervalued

An Introduction

Rosalyn D. Davis and Sharon L. Bowman

As Black women who are reasonably competent at their jobs or respective roles, the authors in this volume have been called on innumerable times to help provide solutions to problems we almost never cause. In theory, there is nothing wrong with seeking out those who may have the information to solve the current problem. However, it is frustrating at best, insulting and confounding at worst, to be sought out for comment, then ignored or told the response is wrong. The few times we are given positions of power to achieve our goals, the pushback from those we are meant to serve can be daunting at best. Even when it is clear that we have the best plan or means to move forward, until it is supported by male or white voices, Black women face hurdles that others do not run into. These hurdles are not unknown, but delay what otherwise might be done efficiently and to the benefit of everyone. We watch in confusion as new initiatives are tackled that clearly had no voices from the people that will be directly impacted by the proposed changes. We also experience what can only be described as schadenfreude when the warnings we politely and diligently gave manifest in highly predictable ways. There is no joy in being right in that way, well there may be a little bit of satisfaction but not joy, because now we will be tasked with the responsibility of fixing what did not have to be broken in the first place.

Black women are routinely out front trying to be proactive instead of reactive to address other issues. Advocating for students, colleagues, the community, the profession, and ourselves so that those who follow us will have smoother transitions into our spaces. We do not want to continue to have the same conversations about protecting our peace, finding mentors in people that look like you even if they don't do the same work, not being afraid to ask your network for connections to someone who can help. Those conversations started for me (Bowman) in the early 1990s and have not stopped in the ensuing years. Either as the mentor or mentee, this work should not be necessary anymore but until the playing field is legitimately level for Black women we will continue to share our knowledge. That insulates the bumpy road and imposter syndrome that Black women face when we enter any number of rooms but it is one small piece of the overall work that Black women repeatedly partake in.

We are normally among the voices, if not the primary voices, encouraging trainings and experiences for our colleagues to ensure that even unintentional mistakes are addressed quickly and without defensiveness. We all make mistakes; learning how to make fewer of them and how to apologize gracefully when we do make them seems like a good thing. However, any new perceived indicator that someone is not as well versed in diversity, equity, and inclusion (DEI) work as they believe themselves to be is met with massive resistance. As a Black woman, I (Davis) am completely aware of what I do not know about a variety of communities. The only way I can get better is by attending trainings, talking to people, and being open to experiences that are different from mine. I think the primary difference is I expect to do those things and people from the dominant community do not expect to do that work as a matter of course. The summer of 2020 being a decided exception when everyone was heavily invested in *White Fragility* and *How to Be an Anti-Racist*, things have slowly returned to normal as we have found ways to work through our pandemic anxiety and return to our regular brand of racism.

That requires that we be ready to continue building out resources and opportunities for diverse individuals so that they see opportunities for themselves in spaces they may not have even considered previously. You will see several authors mention the lack of Black female role models in particular during their early lives. It is difficult to buy into a system where you just do not see yourself existing. Things like Google searches defaulting to white men when you look for professor or young white women when you search for beautiful can wear on your psyche as a young Black person. When will your intelligence, beauty, and drive be recognized if it's not recognized now? Staying in spaces long enough for the next generation and the one after it to see possibilities is necessary, but that toll on Black women can be exhausting. There are a finite number of hours in the day and in some of those hours we need to rest and recharge to continue the good fight. However, we are quite aware that without our continued willingness to be present this may result in someone never having the face they look up to reflect their own brown hues. Opening up our offices and means of communication to conduct the aforementioned mentoring of others who may one day replace us, leading talks about inclusivity, participating in the search process, giving interviews, and attending public functions representing our places of employment are commonplace among every Black woman we know in a variety of settings. We do those things without expecting to be recognized for that unpaid labor, but because we know had it not been offered to us when we were trying to find our own footing as college students and professionals, we likely would not be in the spaces we currently inhabit, which is another reason we felt compelled to offer you these writings.

Each of those things can all be rewarding on their own merits, especially if they are implemented, supported, and succeed as we intended. However, we do not have much recourse if they are not implemented or supported as we intended. Then those well-intentioned offerings become hallmarks of the emotional tax that many Black women pay while trying to make their spaces more nuanced and can become frustrating reminders of the work that still has to be done. The frustration does not come from failed efforts. We have to try and fail in order to improve. The irritation and exasperation comes largely from the fact that no matter how many times we put out those clear fires, fix the pressing concern, and improve the situation drastically, there will be a point that we have to do it all again because instead of moving forward with the next phase of the plan we are halted because we "won." To invoke a phrase that came up often over the last few years, how much winning can we really afford as Black women if we keep having to start all over?

This collection of writings is the result of each of the authors asking each other how we were doing and being honest in our responses to one another. As we were preparing for yet another professional conference cycle, I (Dr. Rosalyn Davis) reached out to my mentor (Dr. Sharon Bowman) as well as colleagues and former students about pulling together to work on a joint proposal. Everyone was very eager to coordinate and started thinking about what was happening in the field, the country, and within the group. Two things became clear immediately. The first was that we were frustrated with needing to be magical to be heard. #Blackgirlmagic is a great hashtag, but it is an exhausting space to inhabit. This is particularly true when the people who run it into the ground have a completely different interpretation than the originators likely had. Sass and humor are great character traits in any demographic, but Black women are also real-life people, not just the plucky sidekick to battle white supremacy with the perfect one liner. The second thing that became clear is that try as we might we just did not have the energy to keep making space for people who refused to listen to what we suggested until a situation had blown up in unanticipated ways.

From the presidential election to our professional spaces, Black women always give strong indications about what their plans are and how they want to achieve them. Yet in 2016, they were indirectly blamed by the sudden rush to break down "identity politics" within the Democratic Party's failure to attract the "forgotten middle American voter" (Gorski et al., 2017; Hardy, 2016; Lilla, 2018). Lilla (2018) went so far as to write a whole book on the failure of identity politics and his lamenting that the Democratic Party would always lose if it didn't remember the disenfranchised white guys, essentially. What Black women knew, and stated, at the time was the loss in 2016 was less about white faces showing up for a party of diverse voters but more about racism (Bacon, 2016). Eight years of a different hashtag, #Blackexcellence, had driven a segment of the country to believe they were somehow suffering because some people were starting to make gains (Reny et al., 2019). The coalition of different voices and goals within the Democratic Party has been buoyed by Black women's activism and committed voting, which makes the party stronger (Abrams, 2019). Additionally, it should be noted that American culture still has a ridiculous mental block about electing, believing, supporting, and empowering overwhelmingly qualified and competent women over petulant men. As we saw with former Secretary of State Hilary Clinton, Senator Elizabeth Warren, and Vice President Kamala Harris's failed presidential campaigns, no woman is good enough for America to let her lead (Anderson, 2017). We saw this again with the confirmation of Brett Kavanaugh to the Supreme Court despite what can only be characterized as a tantrum during his confirmation hearings. We saw a weird paradoxical view of this with the confirmation hearing of Amy Coney Barrett whose only qualification appeared to be that she was not a feminist. Legitimate concerns about each of these candidates were tossed aside, which would not have been possible had either candidate been a Black woman. We know that to be the case because while Judge Ketanji Brown Jackson has more experience than the vast majority of Supreme Court nominees, she is being attacked and viewed as unqualified even though she was supported in previous confirmation hearings by some of the current challengers (Kapur et al, 2022; Joseph, 2022; Blanco & Tan, 2022).

It should be no surprise, then, that if white people will not trust an overly qualified white woman to lead, they will struggle with Black women in leadership positions. We share that now because it illustrates the struggles that are frequently faced by Black women everywhere. Black women continually show up, organize, and get work done when we are the least likely to benefit from that work. We are lauded with accolades, as Stacey Abrams and her fellow organizers were after they helped secure Georgia's two senate seats for the Democratic Party. They were rewarded with more work, though: securing Senator Raphael Warnock's seat in less than a year while also building a large enough base to oust current beleaguered—but still very much committed to the former president—Governor Brian Kemp. Their success has unleashed a mad dash to rewrite election laws to prevent everything from mail-in voting, early voting, same-day voter registration, and handing out supplies to those waiting in long lines. No one has come forward with a plan to assist those women and others as they attempt to secure democracy for everyone but if they fail, we will definitely hear about it and bear the brunt of the populace. This bears repeating as many times as can be repeated. When Black women succeed, everyone benefits. From education to the polls, when Black women are represented in large ways we work to empower everyone else almost universally.

With respect to the commonplace exhaustion shared within the collective, we noticed it was not the result of recent demands on our time and energy. We had not experienced an overwhelming sense of relaxation in years. Recovering from the aforementioned 2016 election and continuing to support our students, colleagues, each other, and ourselves was taxing. Not only because that election exposed in great relief the worst of the "isms" that we knew were lurking beneath some of our society but because there was no respite from it. There was no envelope left to push by the time we got to the 2020 election. We were amid another highly contentious election cycle, a social justice uprising, and rushing unaware into a global pandemic. In the time that has transpired since those events took place, nothing about our collective experience has improved dramatically. In fact, I (Davis) would argue that it has indeed worsened in some regards because of the extra labor costs that frequently are thrust upon Black women in times of confusion. For each win (conviction of the officers who murdered George Floyd and the men who murdered Ahmaud Arbery), we were hit with a substantial loss (no charges being filed for murdering Breonna Taylor, a slow walk to justice for the murder of Atatiana Jefferson, and "shockingly" in my sarcastic voice no conviction in the Kyle Rittenhouse case after he and the judge hung out watching the game in the trial in which the victims could not be called victims). Resisting the psychological onslaught from hearing think pieces, pundits, politicians, and neighbors dehumanize the many intersecting identities we possess was taxing and if we are being transparent: we were just done. Done trying to solve it all, repair it all, patch it up and make it better for anyone that was not us. Even in that moment though, we did not want to sit idly by and let the exhaustion be for naught. Thus, *Overworked and Undervalued: Black Women and Success in America* was born.

We wanted to share the ways in which each of us had been called to service, shared our expertise, rewarded with more work, and asked to work within a system that was not built for us and did not willing share the rules to succeed with those seen as interlopers. This collection of essays will be written from the perspective of current doctoral students, recent mental health graduates, public policy advocates, psychological professionals, and academic psychologists. They will detail one situation per chapter that will include the outcome of that reckoning with race and culture, what we wished our colleagues would have done instead, and how you can take that information for your own and be better with your Black female colleagues as well as yourselves. Ultimately, we wanted to make sure that you were just as committed to being part of the dismantling of systems that harm us all as you are with hearing our voices however briefly while we work on those issues for the good of others as well as ourselves.

HOW SHOULD YOU USE THIS TEXT?

For Administrators

This could be the first step in you understanding why you cannot recruit or retain Black women in your spaces. You will hear from individuals who have experienced your systems as students, trainees, and employees. These essays will discuss the ways in which each woman went into a situation hopeful and excited and may have left that same situation prematurely with disappointment or irritation because a simple thing is what forced them to recalibrate to protect themselves. You have an opportunity to press pause on what you assume the Black women in your spaces need your help with and highlight what they may not feel comfortable to tell you in person. Read it in your cabinet or executive meetings, break down what you have learned, figure out how to implement what you have learned, but above all do not put Black women in your organization on the spot to placate any discomfort you may feel or to "not all jobs" you into feeling better. It is not fair, and we can promise you that you will be accelerating her departure from your spaces.

For Employers and Supervisors

You may see situations you were in with former or current employees. If you do, please pay special attention to what each author suggests could have been done to make their experience better and to make them feel like a valued part of your team. It does not take as much as you think, and salary is not always the panacea that people assume it will be. Having stated that though, do not devalue Black women and the labor that they provide to your spaces. Being Black does not mean she wants to be your DEI team lead or that she has the expertise to do so. Even if she agrees to step up in that regard, compensate—preferably with actual money not your regard—her for the work that is above and beyond her actual job duties. It shows that you value DEI work and you are committed to making change not just managing the optics in your organization.

For Colleagues

You will definitely see yourself in these pages because you are the individuals most of us come into contact with the most. From discounting our accomplishments as a benefit of affirmative action to being legitimately threatened by our success, you have had some of the most pivotal impacts on our functioning in work and educational settings. Before you get defensive, we do not like most of you but when you stumble you fall down hard and just cannot embrace a good old-fashioned apology. They work wonders and are things we should get used to doing regularly anyway. For you, read it, process it, read it again, and then if you are feeling so inclined ask the Black women you know to chat on their time about whatever questions you may have. However, do not get upset if they are not in a place to give you that attention immediately or if they are suspicious of your request. Even if you personally have not been a perpetrator of what we can only refer to as microaggressive violence, someone that looks like you probably has and it likely has made your Black colleagues wary of having open conversations about race with anyone in your space.

For Educators

You will play a unique role in this whole conversation. You are focused, rightfully so, on extending opportunities to diverse populations. The problem is you still look at it from a dominant white view more often than you should. Minor things can make the experience for Black women better. Finding mentors that look like her, inside or outside of your department if necessary, groups that allow her to connect and bond with other Black women, embracing the ways in which her perspective will not match yours but is still inherently valuable, and provide resources for opportunities that ensure her success. That may not be financial all the time but if there is a small ask that the educational environment can sustain figure out how to support it. Turns out alumni can generate donations quickly if projects like this are presented to them. Hear from each of us the ways in which our systems either lifted us up or made us happy to depart and see how you can apply them to your setting.

For the Average White Band

Sorry folks, could not resist there. White men and women who live in environments where your interactions with Black women is limited or regulated to what you see in the media, this book may be confusing for you at first. Each of us has achieved some measure of success by American standards so this may sound like complaining to you. However, as we share these experiences, we want you to consider how many of your family members or friends have had to deal with the same kinds of hurdles with the same level of success. We can readily acknowledge that we are better off than some others, but it does not mean that success is not held onto in a tenuous manner or that it cannot be taken away the moment we become the "problematic" Black woman in a space. "Problematic" or "dangerous" is a catchall for "making our white colleagues uncomfortable." Therefore, if you are just someone white and interesting in reading and learning, just sit down and read in peace. You will likely be in a position at some point to interact with Black women as fellow employees, friends, supervisors, and the like. Just take in what you can, learn about the ways we share some struggles and those that are unique to the Black female experience.

For Black Women

We hope we represent your voices accurately and articulately within these pages. We know we are not going to be able to speak to every experience, but we are going to attempt to unite enough of them so that others can provide you some space from uncomfortable conversations. In the most important ways, we want you to see this as a love letter to each and every one of you that can relate and a call to action for everyone else to ease our collective workload. If we are working together, we can save each other.

When this book was originally conceived, we were amid another highly contentious election cycle and rushing unaware into a global pandemic. In the time that has transpired since those events took place, nothing about our collective experience has improved. In fact, I would argue that it has indeed worsened in some regards because of the extra labor costs that frequently are thrust upon Black women in times of confusion.

REFERENCES

Abrams, S. Y. (2019). E pluribus unum? The fight over identity politics. *Foreign Affairs, 98*(2), 160.

Anderson, K. V. (2017). Every woman is the wrong woman: The female presidentiality paradox. *Women's Studies in Communication, 40*(2), 132–135.

Bacon, Jr., P. (2016, November 13). How the 2016 election exposed America's racial and cultural divides. NBCNews.com. www.nbcnews.com/politics/white-house/how-2016-election-exposed-america-s-racial-cultural-divides-n682306.

Blanco, A. and Tan, S. (2022, March 20). How Ketanji Brown Jackson's path to the Supreme Court differs from the current justices. *Washington Post.* https://www.washingtonpost.com/politics/interactive/2022/ketanji-brown-jackson-school-career/.

Gorski, P., McWilliam, S., Steinfels, P., & Sitman, M. (2017). Beyond identity? Mark Lilla and the crisis of liberalism. *Commonweal*, 13–20.

Hardy, E. (2016). The rise of identity politics. *The Institute of Public Affairs Review, 68*(1 2), 12–15.

Joseph, P. E. (March 23, 2022). The racist, sexist mudslinging at Ketanji Brown Jackson is disgraceful. CNN. https://www.cnn.com/2022/03/23/opinions/ketanji-brown-jackson-hearing-racism-joseph/index.html.

"Judge Ketanji Brown Jackson is one of the most qualified nominees for the Supreme Court Ever." (2022). DemandJustice.org. demandjustice.org/judge-ketanji-brown-jackson-is-one-of-the-most-qualified-nominees-for-the-supreme-court-ever/.

Joseph, P. E. (2022, March 23). The racist, sexist mudslinging at Ketanji Brown Jackson is disgraceful. CNN. https://www.cnn.com/2022/03/23/opinions/ketanji-brown-jackson-hearing-racism-joseph/index.html.

Kapur, S., Tsirkin, and Thorp, F. (March 31, 2022). Why Republicans say they're voting against Ketanji Brown Jackson for Supreme Court. NBCNews. https://www.nbcnews.com/politics/congress/republicans-say-voting-ketanji-brown-jackson-supreme-court-rcna22455.

Lilla, M. (2018). *The once and future liberal: After identity politics*. Harper.

Reny, T., Collingwood, L., & Valenzuela, A. A. (2019). Vote switching in the 2016 election: How racial and immigration attitudes, not economics, explain shifts in white voting. *Public Opinion Quarterly, 83*(1), 91–113.

Chapter 1

Shine Brightly, Diamonds

Kimberly Morris

Dear White people,

We are tired of playing StepNFetchit in the workplace by using humor to ease your discomfort at our competence. African American women are the most educated group (vs. white or black males, white women) and we no longer want to hide our Black Girl Magic under humor to make you feel less threatened by our level of expertise. You label us as "aggressive" and "pushy" when what we are is knowledgeable, capable, and direct.

We have advanced science with web-based software (Janet Bashen). We've gotten patents for inventions related to cataract surgery (Patricia Bath). We've created systems to keep your homes safe (Marie Van Brittan Brown). Yet, if we share our wisdom and knowledge in an open forum, it is only received if done indirectly—while smiling brightly, being jovial, and self-deprecating.

The ironic part about interactions in the business environment is your inability to acknowledge our abilities forces us to assert ourselves in ways that intimidate you. Yes, it becomes the classic self-fulfilling prophecy. Ignoring our brilliance does not diminish our talents but it blocks everyone's capacity to be great.

Sincerely,
Black and Brown people

African Americans do not view the workplace as a place to authentically express themselves (Henry, 2000). I envision African American women writing fictious letters like this one in their heads daily as they enter the workforce because the struggle for identity and acceptance is real. For African American women, the intersection of race, gender, and class can have a negative effect on their career trajectories, which has a direct bearing on their economic, relational, and professional experiences (Smith et al., 2019). Kimberlé Crenshaw (1989, 1991) coined the term "intersectionality" to explain the complex experiences of racism, discrimination, and prejudice that exist for women of color in the workplace.

The experience of intersectionality shaped my professional development, as it has for so many others. My authority figures have always been White. In this way, the consistent and subtle message sent to me was that people like me do not belong in the C-suite. It never dawned on me to be "Department Chair," "Chief," or "Lead investigator" because those roles were reserved for White folks (and White men specifically). The homogeneity of the workplace signaled that the dominant culture was "the right culture" (i.e., "White is right") and that my cultural norms were not acceptable outside of my community. If I began to see myself as a leader, I knew I would run the risk of frightening authority figures who would have perceived me as being "Angry" for making the tough decisions or found me to be "Incompetent" by those who wanted to snuff out my brilliance. Professional rejection would have equaled failure and possibly job loss. In order to succeed, I knew that I needed to get along with the dominant culture, snuff out my Black Girl magic, and match my professional demeanor to their Caucasian style. My Afrocentric ideals were only meant for show; not for tell. My work experience is not unique and these aversive experiences have dire consequences because all workers want to feel valued and need representation in the room where decisions are being made.

Thus, the purpose of this chapter is to discuss the complex machinations of being an African American female in the US workforce due to discrimination and under-representation. This chapter begins with a brief history of the educational hurdles that African American women must first overcome to gain access to the workforce. Next, the dimensions of distinctiveness and belongingness are discussed by exploring the concepts of invisibility and hypervisibility (McCluney & Rabelo, 2019). In the final section, options for helping African American women cope are discussed so we can continue to shine like the diamonds we are even in a workplace that does not truly want us there.

PIPELINE PROBLEMS PROMOTE WORKPLACE HOMOGENEITY

The pipeline from primary school to professionalism was not designed to develop people of color for the workforce. African American students are twice as likely as Caucasian students to drop out of the pipeline before high school graduation (www.equityinhighered.org). Even though the percentages of those earning doctoral degrees is relatively similar by race, fewer African American students, as compared to Caucasian students, earn bachelor's degrees and master's degrees (15% versus 24% and 7% versus 11% respectively; www.equityinhighered.org). Since educational institutions do not adequately train and prepare students of color for professional life, it is no surprise that the workforce lacks diversity and is therefore woefully unprepared for including people of color into the work environment.

As a whole, educational statistics look dismal for people of color. We enter college full of wonder and possibilities but the demands of family life, the lack of resources, the lack of inclusion, and isolation all create roadblocks to eventual graduation. Through mentoring by other women of color, networking, and sheer force of will, African American women continue to outpace their counterparts when it comes to obtaining their degrees. Race/gender data show that African American women are the most educated of any other race/gender group (US Department of Education, National Center for Education Statistics, 2019). Post-degree, African American women are prepared to assume their rightful place in the professional world, which challenges the solace of an all-Caucasian work environment. Discrimination and under-representation create all too familiar obstacles for African American women.

Racism, sexism, and classism ensure that the educational advancements for African American women in the classroom do not translate into occupational success in the workforce. Labor force statistics estimate that African American women comprise 7% of the total workforce but make up 21% of minimum wage workers (www.bls.gov). Only 36% of African American female workers were employed in management and professional-type occupations, which ranks third behind Asian American women and Caucasian women (53% and 45%, respectively; www.bls.gov/opub/reports/race-and-ethnicity/2018/home.htm). Smith et al. (2019) found that African American women were almost non-existent in higher ranking leadership positions. For example, only 1.3% of African American women were found to serve in senior management and executive roles, only 2.2% of Fortune 500 board directors were African American women, and there were reportedly no African American female chief executive officers in the S&P 500. The ultimate question remains: What happens to African American women in the work place that extinguishes the Black Girl Magic and stops them from "running the world" (cue Beyonce's "Run the World")? The answer may lie within the relationships that are (or most often are not) forged in the workplace.

BEING SEEN

McCluney and Rabelo (2019) provide some insight into the vanishing experience of African American women from the workforce. In the article, the authors combined the intersectionality work of Crenshaw with the optimal distinctiveness theory of authors like Brewer and Shore to explain "how Black women are perceived, evaluated, and relegated in organizations." "Distinctiveness" is defined by how distinguishable African American women are from other race/gender groups and is related to aspects of self-esteem and inclusion. "Belongingness" relates to the experience of inclusion in social groups. According to the authors, belongingness is connected to power and privilege and, due to discrimination and under-representation in the workplace, is outside of the scope of the African American worker. Belongingness is greatly influenced by discrimination and oppression. Distinctiveness (low versus high) and Belongingness (low versus high) create four unique experiences for the African American woman: Precarious belonging, Partial belonging, Invisibility, and Hypersensitivity. The dimensions of Invisibility (low distinctiveness, high belongingness) and Hypervisibility (high distinctiveness, high visibility) will be explored for the purposes of this chapter.

INVISIBILITY

Caucasian workers lay ownership to a level of comfort that only exists in homogeneous environments due to white fragility and a sense of entitlement (Erskine et al., 2021). Caucasian workers often respond with hostility when they experience race-related stress due to their lack of skill at interacting with diverse co-workers (Erskine et al., 2021). A rallying cry for every "Karen," as she leverages power and control in diverse settings, is: "I feel threatened." In response to "Workplace Karen's" distress, many African American women attempt to restore peace and harmony by changing authentic things about themselves, which allows White folks to reclaim the sense of authority they feel entitled to.

African American women often wrestle with Invisibility in the workforce because creating and maintaining a less threatening identity has been associated with perceived acceptance by Caucasian co-workers (Dickens & Chavez, 2017). When the identity becomes threatening, the repercussions are swift. Invisibility means that the dominant culture cannot see the African American woman's uniqueness that allows her to experience high belongingness and/or possibly assimilation (McCluney & Rabelo, 2019).

Holland detailed the process of managing distinctiveness and belongingness in her 2019 paper entitled "Don't Dim Your Light." In the article, the author describes how African American women use strategies such as code switching and even hairstyles to increase their sense of belonging and decrease their distinctiveness, which can soothe the sensitive souls of White folks. Code switching (i.e., the practice of shifting from one linguistic code—a language or dialect—to another, depending on the social context or conversational setting; Holland, 2019) is particularly important because language is a powerful tool for bridging connections between people. Open and clear communication is a bridge to creating effective and authentic connections between people. In many cases a woman of color cannot use comfortable language in the workplace. Code switching is exhausting and dehumanizing but more importantly is often never acknowledged by the systems that make it necessary to adapt in this way (Holland, 2019).

Dimming the light of the African American female worker can make her less distinctive while increasing her belongingness. This process can make the African American women appear less threatening to the Caucasian-dominated workplace and can give the illusion of diverse workplace bonds. Dickens and Chavez (2018) provide several examples of the benefits of light dimming for belongingness. These authors interviewed ten African American women who were at the early stages of their careers and asked these women about their workplace experiences. They found that a number of women believed that changing their behavior to be more acceptable to their Caucasian co-workers had belonging benefits. For example, "Harriet," a research participant, stated: "The positive result is that my interaction with various groups of people and cultures has allowed me to become culturally competent. Therefore, I am able to interact with a diverse group of people without being offensive or degrading." Another participant, Jessica, stated: "I think it helps other people become more comfortable around you and you can relate to people more, assimilate more, you can just get along with co-workers more by doing that and it can help you in your career goals because you are identifying with people and connecting with people." These relationships with Caucasian employees can be crucial for career advancement for African American women.

Light dimming can only achieve so much because African American women must still master distinctiveness. Even though "included" in the work environment, African American female workers are often kept out of the informal clubs/groups that form on the job and cause the diverse worker to remain an "outsider" (Smith et al., 2019). Smith et al. (2019) found that African American women were often dismissed and overlooked in the workplace. This "outsider" status prevents African American women from receiving the mentoring and other opportunities that are afforded to "the insiders." As outsiders, African American women lack identity affirmation, lack mentorship, and lack professional opportunity (Apugo, 2019). Dnika et al. (2016) said that African American women pay an "emotional tax" on the job that extends beyond their professional lives and can infringe on their personal lives. According to Dnika et al. (2016), an "emotional tax" is the heightened experience of being different from peers at work because of your gender and/or race/ethnicity and the associated detrimental effects on health, well-being, and the ability to thrive at work. This report shows that an emotional tax can deplete an African American employee's sense of well-being by making her feel that she has to be "on guard," disrupting sleep patterns, reducing their sense of "psychological safety," and diminishing her ability to contribute at work (Dnika et al., 2016).

Researchers such as Holland (2019) and Dickens and Chavez (2018) found that African American women often have to change their authentic selves in order to combat these negative images and attempt to fit into a company that never wanted them there in the first place. The ongoing experience of being an "outsider" and not being able to exhibit authenticity can have long-term consequences. African American women in predominantly Caucasian professional spaces can experience "spirit murder" (i.e., "the cumulative effects of hundreds and thousands of spirit injuries [some major, some minor] which cause a slow death to the psyche, the soul, and the persona"; Erskine, 2021). Hayman et al. (2015) found that exclusionary practices at work resulted in disturbed eating at home among a group of professional African American women. African American women who are early in their careers are particularly susceptible to this type of cost (Dickens & Chavez, 2018; Holland, 2019) because of the "pet status" (i.e., early career professionals, who belong to under-represented groups, are not equal to their senior colleagues and thus are ignored or disregarded for their accomplishments).

If there is a singular message that is the most harmful to the proliferation of Black Girl Magic, it's the following: "I don't see color." At first glance, this message promotes unity but it only serves to disarm African American women. For the longest time, I thought this blind eye to race and culture was a healthy way for diverse peoples to coexist. I now know that the colorless view of the world was another way to disrespect me and those who look like me. Culture matters. A whitewashed world means that only the dominant voice is heard, which leads us back to an old message: "White is right." Although this message makes White people feel comfortable, it keeps people of color from realizing their full potential. It silences cultural pride and the role that diversity has played in making everyone's life better.

The colorless view of the world is also a hypocritical message because race and gender definitely matter in the workplace. Many African American women experience the feeling of being an "outsider" in the workplace. African American women who are early in their careers are particularly susceptible to this type of cost (Dickens & Chavez, 2017; Holland, 2019). Reflecting on my own experiences as a Black professional, I was correct in my third-grade assessment of how things work. It has been "safer" for me to dim my light in White professional environments. Displaying Black Girl Magic has been risky for me because there is very little protection for an African American woman who chooses to be authentic in diverse settings, especially when she is "the only one." The long-term consequence of this decision is that I never truly found my "voice" as a professional. By dimming my light, I continue to second-guess my own skill, talent, and decisions. Unconsciously, I have stayed "in the middle" and have never felt comfortable in a leadership position. That decision has affected my career trajectory and limited my professional options. In reflection, there were several things that could've changed my career confidence and would have propelled me toward my rightful place as an educated Black woman.

HYPERVISIBILITY

Invisibility has its drawbacks such as feeling dismissed and overlooked, paying the emotional tax, experiencing spirit murder, and the inability to be authentic in the workplace. Hypervisibility can also have a negative impact on African American women. Hypervisibility involves high distinctiveness and high belongingness (McCluney & Rabelo, 2019). Caucasian workers have grown accustomed to a workplace that lacks diversity and they tend to become vexed in an environment that involves close, frequent, and cooperative reliance on a workforce composed of diverse members. Due to high distinctiveness, it is estimated that African American women suffer more than any other race/gender group from direct discrimination (Elliott and Smith, 2004) and African American women are almost four times as likely to experience sexual harassment (Cassino & Besen-Cassino, 2018).

The dominant workforce uses distinctiveness labeling to dim the light of African American female workers. African American female workers have been addressed by long-held stereotypes that serve to demean and weaken our professional voice (Smith et al., 2019). Common stereotypes such as "The Angry Black Woman," "The Promiscuous Black Woman," and "The Incompetent Black Woman" undermine the professional expertise of the African American female worker (Apugo, 2019; Wingfield, 2007). Some labels sound empowering but are back-handed compliments for African American women. For example, the label of the "Strong Black Woman" has been used as a badge of honor. However this label can be destructive (Apugo, 2019; Davis & Jones, 2021). African American women have been trained by key family members to embody this image of the strong Black woman to help future generations to survive the racism and discrimination they will receive (Davis & Jones, 2021). Apugo (2019) called this hypervisibility label a "curse" because this seemingly protective label can easily become self-destructive. "African American women are often tasked with maintaining a perpetual shield of strength and perfection that can cause psychological distress and other mental health issues" (Apugo, 2019). These negative caricatures of African American women increase our visibility on the job, which also increases the risk for discriminatory practices and, ultimately, puts us at risk for hostile reactions from Caucasian workers (Kreiger et al., 2006).

I have experienced a number of instances of distinctiveness labeling by the dominant culture that could have resulted in professional demise. The struggle to keep my Black Girl Magic light lit was real. The typical strategy by the dominant culture was to reject my work and frame me as an "Incompetent Woman." For example, I was the only African American person in my post-doctoral program. I was examining race issues but my post-doctoral supervisor, a White woman, rejected all of my research ideas and heavily criticized my writing. She eventually deemed my work as unsatisfactory. She went so far as to challenge my qualifications and would not allow me to continue my training until I produced my doctoral diploma. Although most instances like this were humiliating and confusing, one workplace experience stands out to me because it threatened my livelihood.

At the time, I was the only African American professional on the staff of a small midwestern hospital. Clients of color, in this particular area, were extremely rare. One day, an African American woman was seeking services because she was experiencing an emotional crisis. It was evident to me that her odd behavior clashed dramatically with the cultural values of a God-fearing Christian African American woman. I evaluated her and, using my clinical judgment, I concluded that she was in emergent need of a higher level of care. I made my case to the person in charge, a White woman with significantly fewer years of experience than me. I expected her to accept my assessment so that this affected woman could get the help she so desperately needed. Instead, the White female in charge of admissions quickly dismissed my expertise, even though she had no contact with the client. She rejected the assessment, which effectively deemed the evaluation as "incompetent." I was flabbergasted. When I pointed out the obvious racial undertones of the decision, I was labeled as the "Angry Black Woman" and immediately sent to the department chair. The department chair, a White male, stated that I was running the risk of reprimand because the White female manager stated that she was now "frightened of me"—the rallying cry of every "Karen" when she is trying to restore power with a person of color. Her rallying cry worked. The needs of the client were quickly forgotten because the White authority was now focused on diminishing my light. I was eventually told that I had to apologize to the "Karen" or risk being written up, which would have reflected negatively on my performance and opportunities for employment. Needless to say, I immediately began a job search.

White (2015) found that African American workers were scrutinized more often than their Caucasian counterparts and this scrutiny resulted in poorer performance reviews, lower wages, and even job loss. When an African American woman refuses the status quo, the ultimate "dim your light" event occurs: demotion, public humiliation, and/or firing. The most recent examples occurred at Google when two experienced African American professionals, April Christina Curley and Timnit Gebru, were fired by the company because they spoke out about the institutional racism they were hired to confront (Glaser & Adams, 2020). In a signed petition, Google employees stated: "Instead of being embraced by Google as an exceptionally talented and prolific contributor, Dr Gebru has faced defensiveness, racism, gaslighting, research censorship, and now a retaliatory firing." Once again, the cost of not "dimming your light" and being one's authentic self is risky for African American women. Unfortunately, the onus of responsibility to reduce the racial tension in the workplace falls on the African American female worker so that she can maintain steady and gainful employment.

Dimming the Hypervisibility light is confusing for those of us who were taught by our elders that to be considered equal to a Caucasian peer, you will have to work twice as hard. The concept of being "twice as good" is not just a sentiment shared by family and friends in the African American community. As previously referenced, White wrote about the impact of "being twice as good" in her 2015 *Atlantic* article when she described how African American workers need to be twice as good as their Caucasian counterparts because African American workers are more heavily scrutinized by their employers. The author explained that the increased scrutiny by Caucasian supervisors/bosses increases the risk that the mistakes and errors will be detected. The awareness of the errors can result in a poor evaluation for the African American worker and eventually increases his/her risk of being fired. In fact, the unemployment rate is consistently higher for African Americans than for Caucasians (White, 2015). As a result, African American workers spend a longer time in an unemployed status, which can make getting back into the workforce more difficult. Facts like these make the "dim your light" game a known technique for African American workers. I learned this strategy as a child, even though I didn't know the formal title back then.

I grew up in a predominantly White environment. As far back as I can remember, I was one of only a handful of African American students in my neighborhood, in my class . . . at my entire school! I have always enjoyed education and my family always promoted "learning," so completing high school and going on to college was a given. Positive reinforcement by White authorities and peers played a huge part in shaping me to use the "dim your light" strategy.

I was a smart and social kid in the classroom and I was praised by the Caucasian authority figures (i.e., teachers and administrators) for being pleasant and engaging. Socially, my peers responded favorably to my class clown behavior and negatively to my stellar academic skills, so I toned down the academic prowess and turned up the class clown behavior. For me, positive reinforcement contributed to my decision to conform. I became the loquacious and jovial class clown who made the authority figures and my peers comfortable because I was not a threat. In hindsight, I didn't recognize I was being groomed to dim my light. I just knew that certain behaviors were rewarded and, conversely, certain behaviors were punished. Because I wanted to be liked and I wanted to succeed, I behaved in a manner that supported those two behaviors. I didn't have problems with the White authority and the White authority didn't have problems with me because I did not challenge the power structure that had been created. As a non-threatening African American female, I was left alone to do my work, to tangentially socialize with my peers, and to thrive academically.

Through observational learning, I discovered that shining brightly could be threatening to White authority figures and peers, which resulted in a high cost socially and educationally for African American girls. I watched children of color who were being "authentically themselves" get ostracized, punished, and expelled from school. For example, when I was in third grade, I witnessed the clash of cultures and gender when the only other African American female student in the class complained and rebelled against the system. I remember her expressions of anger that often took the form of yelling at teachers and threatening peers. I wasn't privy to the triggers for the clash; I only witnessed the consequences. As an adult, I recognize that this child needed an advocate; but in this monochromatic environment, that type of support was lacking for this African American child who was struggling. She was eventually ridiculed by the White teachers, rejected by the Caucasian students, and finally expelled from the predominantly White school. This incident was shocking to my nine-year-old psyche, and it further cemented in my child brain that "dimming my light" was the safest course of action. I knew that I didn't want her fate to be my fate and I knew my family would not support an untimely exit from formal education. As a child, I concluded that I had to dim my light in order to succeed because if I chose to challenge the status quo, it most likely would mean failure. That was a sign to me very early on that it's safest to dim my light, stay anonymous, and stay on the good side of the White majority. I had surreptitiously found a solution to the "pipeline problem."

As I ascended into graduate school, I learned that outside cultures didn't respect Black Girl Magic and I learned that there were costs to shining brightly. When I was a young professional, I had an African American friend in a different professional program. I would visit her to discuss psychological concepts. We conversed like African American women do, using our authentic and native voices and our humor to dissect the complicated material. However, unbeknownst to us, the other students complained to the lead investigator that we were "too loud" and "unprofessional" because we were acting in ways that were common to us and to our culture but foreign to them and their culture. They assumed that we were "playing around" and "not taking graduate school seriously." Our expertise was eventually called into question. When the excellent work spoke for itself, the lead investigator praised us for the level of craftsmanship. Even though the work was impressive, we opted not to work together in her workspace again. The costs of being ourselves were too high and we learned a powerful message that day: "Sit still, look pretty."

Another salient "light dimming" experience also occurred in graduate school. Once again, I was "the only"; all other graduate students in my laboratory were White as was my grad school advisor and the middle-aged female office manager. Our advisor was a pleasant White woman who rarely came to the laboratory. Our daily interactions were mostly with the office manager, a curmudgeonly white woman. As is common with graduate school, the days were long and the work environment was high stress. Just like my fellow students, my day-to-day demeanor reflected the circumstance I was involved in. I was stressed and tired and not "into" small talk. One day I was summoned into my advisor's office because she wanted to correct my "rude" behavior. I looked at her confused. Apparently, the White office manager reported me to the advisor because I hadn't been saying "good morning" to her. My advisor went on to say that my intense behavior made the White office manager feel "uncomfortable" (the Karen rallying cry) and that I needed to be more pleasant and say "good morning" to help the office manager "feel better." This particular conversation has haunted me since the day it happened. I can only surmise that I was singled out because I was acting the role of my authentic self (i.e., a stressed out graduate student) and not as the class clown. Microaggressions like these serve to dim the light of those of us who are trying to be authentically ourselves. Knowing what I know now, I would challenge my advisor by pointing out her unacceptable behavior, alerting her to the level of disrespectful she was showing to me. My needs had been dismissed to restore comfort to the majority. My authenticity was diminished without any recourse for me because my ally had sided against me. At the time, the power differential between my advisor and myself, as a student, was too great and I didn't have the language to explain how her reprimand had diminished me.

PROTECTING THE SOULS OF BLACK WOMEN

Regardless of whether it is invisibility or hypervisibility, racism and discrimination take a toll on the souls of African American professional women. The remedy is complex because work and home are separate dimensions for African American women (Smith et al., 2019). This means that each experience requires a different set of coping strategies for mitigating the negative consequences of intersectionality.

At work, role-modeling, developmental advice, and advocacy by mentors and sponsors are key (Smith et al., 2019). I was fortunate to have an African American woman as a mentor for a few years during both my undergraduate and graduate careers. This woman had a profound effect on me. Although she was not in my department, this highly skilled professional African American woman provided me with much-needed guidance professionally and personally. She reminded me of my strengths and talents and did not reinforce the class clown persona I had perfected. She told me to apply for scholarships that funded my education. She critiqued my professional writing and encouraged me to conduct presentations. She encouraged me to have a voice that spoke power, strength, and confidence and reminded me that any sense of inferiority I encountered was the responsibility of the other and not my burden to carry. This investment was short-lived. She left early in my graduate training. My heart sank and my career trajectory changed. I completed my education based on the course that she had set for me but I have often wondered what my career would have looked like if she had remained and/or other African American mentors had been available.

African American women need allies from the dominant culture in the workplace if they are to transition to belongingness status (Smith et al., 2019). I have been very fortunate to have a number of dominant culture professional mentors throughout my career who provided me with details on how to succeed. One high-ranking professional would simply have lunch with me twice per year to "just chat." The information shared in those informal lunches changed my career trajectory. She would comment on ways I could build my professional brand and leverage my experiences to make a difference. One professional called me weekly to "check in." He made insightful comments about how to navigate professional relationships. He would send manuals that he thought would deepen my expertise on therapy topics and he would make professional connections with me if he thought they would advance my career. These professional relationships have been invaluable for success in the workplace.

At home, emotional support, self-care, and spirituality are staples (Hall et al., 2012). Williams et al. (2020) said that African American women need "a safe space to simply exist as Black women" and that safe space is usually in the presence of other African American women. My saving grace has always been my African American female peers. From the first day of my undergraduate career to my present day as a professional, I have been surrounded by Black Girl Magic. These brilliant and beautiful women have supported me with kind words and gestures and with practical tips and solutions. I have tried to do the same for them. Being able to share ideas freely without being judged meant the world to me. We support each other as we trod along our professional paths. We gain strength from each other's success and learn from each other's mistakes. We nurture each other, which allows us to shine brightly. We recognize the brilliance in each other and often honor that brilliance by recommending each other for jobs. For example, my closest friend from undergrad recommended me for a tenure track position at her university. We continue to encourage each other to grow professionally. We recommend each other for career-broadening experiences like being editors of professional journals. We keep each other informed about relevant topics for funding. There is no jealousy, there is no backstabbing; there is only nurturing and support. In small ways and in large ways, my African American sisters have told me to continue to shine brightly and to never let anyone dim my light.

My experience is not unique. Many researchers have found that emotional support has been particularly valuable to African American women because of the lack of formal professional guidance and/or mentors who possess any power to advance their careers (Bailey et al., 1996; Erskine, 2021). In several studies, African American women identified family members as their most important source of emotional support (Bailey et al., 1999; Hall et al., 2012; Smith et al., 2019). For example, Smith et al. (2019) estimated that 39% of their professional women relied on the support of parents and spouses. Smith et al. (2019) stated that African American women in executive positions "relied on their personal contexts to draw on the fortitude for striving in predominantly White institutions and industries." The support of friends and family can also have practical applications for African American professional women. Elliott and Smith (2004) describe how women, in general, engage in self-removal from the workplace by voluntarily leaving the workforce for marriage and motherhood. Bailey (1999) and Smith (2004) stated that African American women may experience a work-home conflict because they often take on more responsibilities at home. As a result, African American women may need the practical support of these at-home networks to accomplish the work of both work and home.

CONCLUSION

African American women are the most educated of all race and gender groups. Despite their numerous academic accomplishments, these women continue to experience a number of racist and discriminatory practices in the workplace. To combat the negativity of hostile environments, these women can choose a commonly practiced neutralizing strategy, "dim their light," which can serve to make their Caucasian co-workers feel more comfortable with a diverse workforce and can lessen the scrutiny of African American women by those in power. "Dim your light" as a strategy can positively effect cross-racial co-worker relationships but can have significant negative personal effects on the psyche of African American women, if over-used. African American women continue to thrive despite the challenges by recharging with emotional and practical support from each other. The willingness of African American women to persevere ultimately means that workspaces continue to be diverse and representative of race, gender, and class. Diversity without inclusion is tokenism, however (Snell, 2017).

The goal is, therefore, not simply to have African American women counted in the workplace. The goal is to integrate African women into workspaces, thus creating an inclusive environment where contributions of African American women are respected and highly regarded. There are many benefits of an inclusive workplace and, in such an environment, not only will African American women benefit, the workplace benefits, as a whole. Inclusive workplaces have lower turnover rates, increased productivity, and higher morale (www.naceweb.org/diversity-equity-and-inclusion/best-practices/the-benefits-of-creating-an-inclusive-work-culture/). According to *Women in Tech*, an inclusive environment results in increased productivity and increased creativity because workers feel empowered (www.womenintech.co.uk/4-key-benefits-of-inclusion-in-the-workplace). Thus, promoting inclusivity for African American women means overall benefit for all involved. This is the ultimate win-win situation.

REFERENCES

Apugo, D. (2019). A hidden culture of coping: Insights on African American women's existence in predominately White institutions. *Multicultural Perspectives, 21*(1), 53–62.

Bailey, D., Wolfe, D., & Wolfe, C. (1999). The contextual impact of social support across race and gender: Implications for African American women in the workplace. *Journal of Black Studies, 26*(3), 287–307.

Cassino, D., & Besen-Cassino, Y. (2019). Race, threat and workplace sexual harassment: The dynamics of harassment in the United States, 1997–2016. *Gender Work Organ., 26*, 1221–1240.

Crenshaw, K. (1989). Demarginalizing the intersection of race and sex: A Black feminist critique of antidiscrimination doctrine, feminist theory and antiracist politics. *The University of Chicago Legal Forum, 140*, 139–167.

Crenshaw, K. (1991). Mapping the margins: Intersectionality, identity politics, and violence against women of color. *Stanford Law Review, 43*(6): 1241–1279.

Davis, S. M., & Jones, M. K. (2021). Black women at war: A comprehensive framework for research on the Strong Black Woman. *Women's Studies in Communication, 44*(3), 301–322.

Dickens, D. D., & Chavez, E. L. (2017). Navigating the workplace: The costs and benefits of shifting identities at work among early career U.S. Black women. *Sex Roles, 78*, 760–774.

Dnika, J. T., Thorpe-Moscon, J., & McCluney, C. (2016). Emotional tax: How Black women and men pay more at work and how leaders can take action. Catalyst.Org.

Elliott, J. R., & Smith, R. A. (2004). Race, gender, and workplace power. *American Sociological Review, 69*, 365–386.

Erskine, S. E., Archibold, E. E., & Bilimoria, D. (2021). Afro-Diasporic women navigating the Black ceiling: Individual, relational, and organizational strategies. *Business Horizons, 64*, 37–50.

"Four key benefits of women in technology." www.womenintech.co.uk/4-key-benefits-of-inclusion-in-the-workplace.

Glaser, A., & Adams, C. (December 2020). Second top Black female Google employee says she was recently ousted. NBCNews. www.nbcnews.com/tech/tech-news/second-top-black-female-google-employee-says-she-was-ousted-n1252277.

Hall, J. C., Everett, J. E., & Hamilton-Mason, J. (2012). Black women talk about workplace stress and how they cope. *Journal of Black Studies, 43*(2), 207–226.

Hayman, L. W., McIntyre, R. B., & Abbey, A. (2015). The bad taste of social ostracism: The effects of exclusion on the eating behaviors of African-American women. *Psychology & Health, 30*(5), 518–533.

Henry, A. (2000). Thoughts on black women in the workplace: A space not intended for us. *Urban Education, 35*(5), 520–524.

Hodson, G., Ganesh, N., & Race, T. (2021). Double-pronged bias against black women: Sexism and racism (but not right-wing ideology) as unique predictors. *Canadian Journal of Behavioural Science / Revue Canadienne Des Sciences Du Comportement.* https://doi-org.proxyko.uits.iu.edu/10.1037/cbs0000227.supp (Supplemental).

Holland, N. (June 28–29, 2019). Don't dim your light. *Medical Marketing & Media.*

Jones, M. K., Leath, S., Settles, I. H., Doty, D., & Conner, K. (2021). Gendered racism and Depression among Black women: Examining the roles of social support and identity. *Cultural Diversity and Ethnic Minority Psychology.*

Krieger, N., Waterman, P. D., Hartman, C., Bates, L. M., Stoddard, A. M., Quinn, M. M., Sorensen, G., & Barbeau, E. M. (2006). Social hazards on the job: Workplace abuse, sexual harassment, and *racial* discrimination—a study of Black, Latino, and

White low-income women and men workers in the United States. *International Journal of Health Services*, (36)1. 51–85.

McCluney, C. L., & Rabelo, V. C. (2019). Conditions of visibility: An intersectional examination of Black women's belongingngess and distinctiveness at work. *Journal of Vocational Behavior, 113*, 143–152.

Smith, J. W., & Joseph, S. E. (2010). Workplace challenges in corporate America and differences in black and white. *Equality, Diversity and Inclusion: An International Journal, 29*(8), 743–765.

Smith, A. N., Watkins, M. B., Ladge, J. J., & Carlton, P. (2019). Making the invisible visible: Paradoxical effects of intersectional invisibility on the career experiences of executive Black women. *Academy of Management Journal, 62*(6), 1705–1734.

Snell, T. (2017). Tokenism: The result of diversity without inclusion. Medium.Com. https://diversityforward.medium.com/tokenism-the-result-of-diversity-without-inclusion-460061db1eb6.

White, G. (October 7, 2015). Black workers really do need to be twice as good. The Atlantic. www.theatlantic.com/business/archive/2015/10/why-black-workers-really-do-need-to-be-twice-as-good/409276/.

Williams, Q., Williams, B. M., & Brown, L. C. (October 15, 2020). Exploring Black girl magic: Identity development of Black first-gen college women. *Journal of Diversity in Higher Education*. Advance online publication.

Wingfield, A. H. (2007). The modern mammy and the angry black man: African American professionals' experiences with gendered racism in the workplace. *Race, Gender & Class, 14*(1/2): 196–212.

Chapter 2

For the Black Girls with Difficult Names and Big Personalities, You Are Seen and Loved

Rosalyn D. Davis

I want to paint a picture for you. I will borrow heavily for the storytelling stylings of one Miss Sophia Petrillo. Picture it, United States of America, it's the year 2005 and a young Black woman is on the hunt for a full-time job after being nearly finished with her doctoral degree in counseling psychology. She is intelligent, skilled, well-trained, and should have a ton of options in her pursuit. Especially as she was gifted with those racially neutral names that would still be mispronounced and misspelled throughout her lifetime (Bertrand & Mullainathan, 2003; Kline et al., 2021). However, after going on the market she only landed two strong interviews with other offers coming well after she had taken a position. Knowing what I know about the hiring cycle now, I was likely in pile two of the applicants and after the first pile didn't work out, they came knocking. That's lovely. At least I was still considered, right? Well not really, because believe me on paper I am borderline flawless. I do all the things and have done so since I was being guided by someone who also did all the things. I was flown out to one interview and drove to another because it was close. One interview was warm and friendly, and I met with people well above my pay grade who were almost begging me to take the job. The other interview was less warm and less friendly and when I left the only thing I was pretty sure of was I would not be taking that position even if it was offered. It was offered and I didn't take it. What both of them were very clear about was how they were failing in some areas and how I would be able to assist them, hopefully.

The position I ended up taking told me up front they were failing in the work they wanted to do with Black students. The center had not had a Black psychologist on staff in five years and the students were suffering. Now you might think, why walk into that situation? What in the world would you gain from that experience? Well, you would need to understand that the scenario I described had been repeated in nearly every professional and educational environment I had except two—my undergraduate and doctoral studies. Those were one of the few times in my life that I can honestly say I just got to be "an" amazing Black girl instead of "the" amazing Black girl. It's not a distinction that seems all that stark, but when you are one of only versus having strength in numbers then things are decidedly different for you. It's not something that you can easily quantify, but being embraced as a whole person instead of just a statistic was a blissful moment that ultimately did help me succeed in all the other roles I would play later (Shippie & Debb, 2019). As I walked into my office late that summer, I knew what to expect in one sense and was altogether unprepared in another sense and would watch an old cycle play out again. Before I cover that experience though I want to start at the beginning of this ever-present two-step in my life.

LET'S DANCE

Learning the Basics

As other authors have noted in their chapters, I was one of the smart Black kids from the minute I entered the school system nearly a year early. I was an only child for a long time. I also had two nerdy college-educated parents who invested in my learning well before kindergarten was a thing. My father let me take apart things (radios and walkie talkies) and put them back together, which eventually led to his summer math assignments for me before I could go out to play. My mother was trained as a special education teacher who didn't have anyone else to talk to most days except me, so my vocabulary and writing was probably stronger than it should have been at four. I also think she was tired of me being a wee tiny ever-questioning tot after my brother was born, which is why she kind of forced the school to let me in early even though I was one of the late birthday kids. A few mandatory tests later, and two things happened. First, no one ever questioned my mother on my intelligence level ever again because I obliterated those mandatory tests. Second, I realized how much of an anomaly those scores appeared to my teachers. I was either met with shock and awe upon entering a new grade level because my name and test scores did not scream young Black woman or met with hand-wringing teachers who bemoaned that I wasn't working harder or outperforming my classmates by more of a margin. I will be the first to admit that I did not work as hard as I could have in K–12, but I also did not have to work that hard. There was nothing challenging about the material presented. My challenge then, as it can be now, was to find my tribe and learn about something that had nothing to do with Texas history.

There were never a large number of Black children in any school I was in save a year or two, and most of those kids were not with me after third grade. We were tracked into TAG (talented and gifted), regular courses or special education classes after third grade. When I was still in the predominantly Black school my TAG class had ten beautiful bright Black faces who were equally nerdy. We had a very cool, and my only in the K–12 system, Black male teacher who knew everything it seemed like and encouraged us to explore what we wanted as long as we delivered a project by the end of the semester. By fifth grade, after a move to one of the better predominantly white districts, I entered into what would become a common occurrence for me going forward. I was the only or one of less than a handful of Black faces. That resulted in awkward conversations about race, racism, my hair, my facial features, *Roots*, and why there were not more Black kids in the space especially because I was the only one that had problems with any of our lessons. I did have the obligatory lessons during Black History Month that covered the same five or ten faces and filled in with pivotal moments of Black history that seemed separated from Black people. I learned about Blackness and my culture, history, and other luminaries outside of the schoolhouse thanks to my parents and those perpetual summer reading lists. If I hadn't, I may not have understood that I was not an aberration to the status quo. There had been and would continue to be intelligent Black men and women who gifted the world with their talents despite what my textbooks and teachers had access to in their training.

I didn't know terms like structural inequalities, systemic racism, redlining, or the fact that education funding was based on property taxes and the property taxes in Black and Brown neighborhoods are routinely suppressed, which in turn reduces funding for Black and Brown schools. What I did know is we weren't covering Black culture enough, and we helped stage a walkout, complete with alerting the local news media, before our school let us proceed with the planned assembly. We had no Black teachers of any kind and our boys football team got trading cards for losing in the playoffs, but our girls volleyball team continued their multiyear domination with little to no recognition. What I did know, as well, is that my white classmates were blaming affirmative action for not getting into Brown or Vassar or in some cases not even being able to get an application from Smith without recognizing that maybe some of those Black, Brown, and Asian faces were legitimately smarter than them. I was able to donate my applications to Brown and Smith to the less fortunate folks in my class because I had been getting them because I took the PSAT, and they were sitting in a box that I had marked "do not apply." I'm not sure if that made me more or less popular with those folks but it did make me giggle. I have always been able to point out the problems and try to develop reasonable solutions to those problems. What I didn't know as a slightly militant high school student was that this skill set would be a regular part of my life indefinitely. However, those moments contributed to me seeking out an HBCU, historically Black college or university, for my undergraduate training. I needed a few years in a place that everyone looked like me and my pursuits were not viewed from the lens of my skin color.

Let me just say I will not belabor the experiences I had in undergrad or during my doctoral studies. Those moments were almost restful in comparison to what faced me outside of those environments. I got to bloom and be challenged and learn new skills and become a more confident version of myself. I would need all of that to deal with the moments in between those experiences and afterward. Both environments were full of people that held me accountable while also making sure that I was aware of how amazing I may have been or applauding the work that I was doing. Sometimes we say things like you need a good cheerleader in your corner in order for you to achieve your greatness. Well, I had those cheerleaders and mentors in each of those places. They are still near and dear to me now and contribute to my own mentoring process now. We need people to push us as well as celebrate us, and those folks keep me invested in this work as we speak. I specifically mentioned two training points but have not addressed the one in the middle yet and let's just say it was a different experience entirely.

Name that Tune

When I was working on my master's degree, the previous training would need to kick back in so that I could survive. The city I was in was very diverse, so I perhaps had my guard down when I shouldn't have. I may have been lulled into complacency because I easily found another Black female mentor, most of my interactions were with enlightened men and women, and the educator in charge of my school was a Hispanic man. It should have been another time of peace, but a well-meaning albeit clueless instructor was at a loss for words when the room of largely Black and Brown faces did not know the beat of the song *I Wish I Were in Dixie* because we had to learn that in school right. Well, no, we were not lamenting how we were really close to the Mason Dixon line in any K–12 school I was in thankfully.

This was followed up with a genealogy assignment that several of us explained would not fit on a sheet of paper if the instructor wanted to be able to read it because we came from large families. We showed up with posterboards that were not collected at the end of the night and just made us cranky. However, the ultimate moment of "this cannot be my life" happened when this same instructor explained that when working with minoritized clients—especially Black clients—we needed to maintain eye contact the entire time otherwise it would be seen as disrespectful. When I and other Black students asked for clarification, they just repeated their statement, and we had to strongly disagree for the sake of our classmates. I guess our reaction was strong enough that they went to check with my mentor and upon hearing that she agreed with us the instructor did apologize. I admit I wasn't expecting that but also wasn't expecting to hear about Dixie either so all in all it was a bit of a wash at the end. Other incidents did arise, but I learned to work with the other students of color to support each other and make adjustments that made sense for us as well as would help people that looked like us in the long run. I am being brief in those historical references so I can address what that has looked like professionally because that has been an amazingly diverse and maddening array of experiences at this point in my life. So clearly the need to name and address the thing, whatever the thing was, had become part of my makeup well before my employer told me that they had been falling in one arena. It made it much easier to take the position and appreciate the role I needed to play while there.

This Beat Feels Familiar

I walked into that job in the late summer understanding two things that were really gifted to me because of previous experiences. It would be hard for me to do exactly what I was hired to do because people often feel inadequate when they do not know how to handle something themselves and they in turn may throw up roadblocks to you achieving the stated objectives. Even when those objectives are benefitting everyone involved, if someone felt uncomfortable about what they didn't know or were unable to contribute to solving the problem then it would become a bigger different problem. I was also aware that my presence in that space would lend everyone else some cover in the work they would do with Black students going forward. It didn't mean they were bad at working with those students before I arrived by any means. However, a Black face in most spaces implies that the people we're working with are more enlightened than other spaces with no Black or Brown faces. A number of studies have noted that having a more diverse staff does lead to more inclusion if those individuals are given a chance to help move the environment forward. In some cases, just the presence of one point of diversity can increase morale, profits, and reduce the opportunity for mismanagement.

Before I move on, I have to say my colleagues were lovely people and I don't recall a moment in which my Blackness explicitly was an issue in that role. I actually have to give my boss credit for acknowledging that our location didn't actually afford me the opportunity to bask in Black only spaces very often. If I did not have my sorority sisters in the area, I would have been largely isolated from Black individuals for nearly a decade. In ways that raised the profile of my position, I was not only allowed but encouraged to be the Black face for our collective. That meant serving on the University Diversity Committee, training graduate students on issues related to diversity, and intervening when the undergraduate chapter of a historically Black sorority lost a member were all tasks I could readily do without hesitation. Other things became more a challenge considering why I was hired in the first place. I couldn't just work with the Black kids that came in no matter how much they wanted to work with me. I couldn't be the only one doing the outreach to the Black and Brown organizations because then no one else on staff would be known by those groups. I couldn't start Black-focused groups because who would run them if I wasn't available. It was a weird dance that I will admit to finding jarring. How could I do my job if I couldn't do my job? I kept up my part of the two-step until I got to meet the therapist that I replaced.

We chatted in my office privately when he came to visit the area with his family. He deliberately stopped in on a day that he knew I would be there, he checked with the boss, and wanted to make sure that he "laid eyes on me." For everyone that knows, you will immediately probably be nodding your heads right now. For those that don't know, he wanted to talk to me alone and make sure I was okay. That is one of those things that lots of people from minoritized groups will do. Not because we think anyone is doing anything in particular but because we know that being the only person in your professional space is isolating and can be exhausting. At the time of his visit, I think I had been there for five or so years. He was glad I had not left yet but also encouraged me to consider when it would be time to leave. Apparently, we had been hired with the same goals and once he realized he would not be able to fully achieve them within the confines of that position, he went to find a space that would let him do that. He was friendly. We joked for quite a while. He gave me his contact information and encouraged me to stay in touch but reminded me to be looking at the clock so that I did not overstay my time there. That sat with me for a long time, but I was still in my guarded optimist stage so didn't want to give up the fight.

When a different colleague, the only other person of color on staff, also left I should have followed them out. We shared almost no commonalities, but we could talk and giggle about things together and we could support one another as well. Within a few years I was out as well. I cannot say I had achieved the goals for which I was hired but I was exhausted. The environment had shifted in the time since I was hired in a lot of ways that were not healthy, but I still felt bad for abandoning "my kids" as I had come to see the Black and

Brown students. This is also one of the struggles Black women face when we are in positions that ask us to address inequities without the support or power to impart lasting change. How long do we stay before we give up on the idealized goals for our position if it is clear they can't be achieved? Who will suffer if we are no longer in a position to assist the people that look like us? When will someone be able to replace us? Will someone even be given the chance to replace us?

My next position was not much better, but that was because we were not talking about making change at all. That stint was just focused on billing and creating a schedule with people who did not want a ton of treatment and definitely didn't want it from a young Black woman with slowly graying hair. When I brought that up to the hiring manager, it was like they just realized why none of the other minoritized therapists had stayed with them very long. We were working with elderly, largely white, clients in an area that was only recently diversifying so I was likely an affront to multiple points of experience for them. None of that was taken personally but it wasn't going to work if people couldn't even be in the same room as me. Thankfully, more opportunities were coming and had one paid better I may not have left it. It was the one time that I got to bask in my Blackness professionally and connected with my students who saw me as a role model who was invested in them. Turns out working-class white students need a cheerleader as well and I can be that when we can have open conversations about all the things that impact our communities. They were intrigued and just wanting to get to the next part of their lives and saw education as their way up and out of the situations they were stuck in at that point. We figured out how to do statistics in Excel when the campus wouldn't pay for SPSS. I let them write and present on topics that were personally impactful to them, and we took care of each other in those courses. I loved those students and that opportunity. It led me to the next one I will discuss in depth, but I will say that I had the same struggle leaving them as when I left my Black and Brown kids. Anyone can teach a course or be a therapist, not everyone is willing to invest in the students who don't see themselves where you are willing to take them.

When I went back into the job market, I assumed that with my now decade's worth of professional experience that I would find a new job in the area I wanted to with no hesitation. That wasn't entirely true, but I did land a few interviews around the same time again. One moved much faster than the other one though and I had an offer in hand before the other had scheduled in-person interviews. This time there was no discussion of what was lacking with regard to diversity training or recruitment. I assumed that eventually, given my materials and my areas of interest, opportunities to explore that would naturally arise. I assumed incorrectly.

What I hadn't realized about academia, after working in the student affairs side of things, was how long it took to make curricular changes even as others are asking to expand things. This was really confusing to me as well given my educational background at an HBCU, HSI, and a very progressive PWI. While I think I offered to teach courses about diversity within psychology within a few semesters of my arrival, it wasn't until an external panel said no you really need regular diversity offerings before they became part of my course load. I honestly would have been happy to count that as a win as I was able to add three different diversity courses to the undergraduate curriculum in short order. The department was happy, students were happy, and we looked like we were ahead of the curve as others scrambled to catch up to what we were doing. I also made sure to add aspects of DEI to each class that it was appropriate for so it wasn't restricted to one optional class that students could take. Let me be clear, I don't think anyone was averse to having the classes on the schedule, but this world makes shifts slowly and we tend to focus on the has to get done instead of should be done.

Let's Pick a New Song

Much like the time of my first professional position, I've been invited to serve on different committees, projects, and groups related to diversity, equity, and inclusion. What is different, at least for me, is that I found another layer to my voice in that time span. Instead of hoping a gentle nudge or less forceful conversation will impart change, I am one of the full-throated commentors who refuses to allow bad decisions to be made without going on record that they are bad decisions. That can draw some unwanted attention, like when we focused on whether or not we would we join the ranks of campuses with required annual diversity training. Even though it wasn't my proposal or idea, the discussions quickly made it a thing I was pushing. If I'm honest, I was okay with that as well. I watched as students and colleagues left our space because we were not addressing diversity broadly. The same few faculty and staff attended each DEI training every year. Consistency is great if it is imparting change but, in this case, it resulted in the same few folks doing a lot of the heavy lifting and everyone else appearing to be okay because at least something was being done. We did pass the training requirement, opened up a new multicultural center, are working on self-paced DEI modules to provide a series of trainings for those who cannot make the hard scheduled events, relaunched our campus climate survey, and are forming an affinity group. I should be basking in wonderful happy feelings right now but being perfectly honest I'm exhausted.

Those achievements came together all at once but took years of work to achieve. It took multiple voices over those multiple years to build to enough of a rumble that it convinced everyone else to get on board. I feel bad for other colleagues at different institutions who marvel at the work we've done because they are still in the building capital portion of this work, and they don't always have the same amount of support from other minoritized colleagues to force the issue. To be clearer, we do have to force the issue because no one sees themselves as part of the problem even when we can point to clear moments of them definitely not being part of the solution. That distinction matters too. People know, but students in particular know, who is safe and who will help them if they are struggling with something. I, and other colleagues, enjoy being part of the safety net for minoritized individuals, but that comes at a price. I am sure that I have expended some of my good capital by having to repeatedly name the thing so we could address it so we could transition from idea to beneficial movement. However, if I cannot name the thing we end up stuck and reacting to the next thing instead of being prepared for it and being able to pivot into positive change. As I mentioned at the end of the previous paragraph, it also means that I am beyond tired. Yes, the pandemic played into that but my reward for being skilled in this area is more work to do both in my job and external to it.

I serve now, and have served in the past, on several regional and national committees or boards outside of my full-time position. Part of that work is always to address the diversity blind spots. When I say addressing blind spots, just staying with race and ethnicity would be easy but gender, SES, religion, country of origin, family, sexuality, and much more are still present as well. Just asking the question leads to new kinds of work that is all important but is not always welcomed. Helping to craft new diversity statements, looking at how we evaluate diverse candidates, how we can diversify membership in a group, and providing mentorship to minoritized individuals is not particularly stressful work, but it is one of the first moments of resistance I am likely to see if a group is not quite ready for the changes to take place. From a psychological perspective, they are likely in that contemplation stage of change. Understanding it needs to happen but not always ready for the discomfort that comes along with (1) not knowing how to impart that change on their own and (2) reluctant to do much to disturb the status quo. The upside for me, though, is usually there's enough folks who are poised for change to get us from contemplation to tangible change. The other upside for me is once that change is imparted, and frustrations may be at their highest with me for dragging stragglers along for the ride, I usually get to leave. I don't have to continue fighting for slow change and if they don't continue to advance then I can happily say that I had no control over that stagnation or regression. That helps me make peace with what could have been done if we had time to build the groundswell as I have in my full-time work. It doesn't mean that the work was anywhere near being completed though and that is a shame.

This work, my work, ultimately is one of starts and fits. As we have addressed several things in terms of DEI, there are still areas that we are struggling to accomplish, and we have to decide if we continue to flesh out the work we have started or jump into totally new areas that need attention. Do we take one project to its possible conclusion or switch gears entirely? If we switch gears, does the other work get left behind or do we have time to come back to it? These will always be the questions if you are the person who is pressing for change while also trying to protect your peace. There will be days when all of it seems overwhelming and not enough and then something will happen to allow you to reclaim your patience, presence, and to persevere.

This One's for My Girls

This chapter has been written over the course of many months and that is probably to its benefit. Many things have come up and deserve a bit of attention that connects to me and that is wholly separate from my experience. I mentioned Associate Justice Brown Jackson at the beginning of this book. I respect her calm in the face of foolishness and know that I likely wouldn't have had it if my qualifications had been under assault from toddlers. I haven't referenced other Black women who became or have been targets of conversation or derision because I did not have the emotional range available to me to do so. When Black women try to change a narrative, situation, or the world, there is almost always unnecessary pushback. When Dr. Timnit Gebru wrote a paper highlighting the dangers of large language models, models her employer at the time was employing, she was painted as producing less than satisfactory scholarship as cause for her unexpected exit (Hao, 2020). The fact that she is a leading scholar on diversifying AI so that it recognizes people of color was not valuable enough to keep her employed, or her reputation unblemished, when her employer had enough. President Joseph Biden's new press secretary created a series of firsts, which to be honest we should be past in 2022 but as we just got the first Black female justice of the Supreme Court it is clear that Black women still have so many more gains to make, including a torrent of negativity for stating positions largely shared by the American public on topics like racism (Levine, 2022). That isn't to say that her predecessor was immune from criticism but the massive dog whistle that these critiques are alluding to are clearly based in misogynoir. If that word is unfamiliar to you it represents the unique relationship between misogyny and racism directed specifically at Black women and can come from anyone about any topic (Bailey & Trudy, 2018). Or remember back when Michelle Obama wanted kids to actually eat food that was good for them and to them and people freaked out because ketchup would no longer be included as a fruit or vegetable serving (Oliphant, 2011; Gold & Hennessey, 2013). I could spend days recounting insane stories about Black women and the ways in which we are routinely demeaned in this country for the choices we make. Large and small, we are discussed, mocked, and then copied in entirely too many ways. From our hair choices to our love lives, nothing seems to be off limits.

Pop star Ciara and tennis legend Serena Williams have both married men who seem to love them dearly. Neither has been applauded for this. Ciara's husband, a millionaire football player named Russell Wilson, has been called everything but his name for overtly loving his wife and taking care of his family. Serena's husband had the nerve to be a white guy marrying one of the most well-known Black female athletes on the planet. In exchange for that, he's had to watch people attack his wife for marrying a white man and calling her a number of disparaging names that I will not repeat right now. And then there's Lori Harvey, who I admit only seems to be famous because her stepfather is famous, who is receiving negative press for dating like men do, basically. She hasn't settled down and keeps dating famous men. Men admittedly she'd have more exposure to because of her family. If you had missed any of those stories maybe you've heard of these two. Vice President Kamala Harris was attacked while campaigning for the Democratic presidential nomination about an alleged affair she had with a married man to ascend to power. It was nonsensical and without merit, but it made bigger news than any of her policy decisions (Reuters, 2021). There was also supposition in the Black blogosphere that the only reason Associate Justice Ketanji Brown Jackson was ultimately confirmed was because she too had married a White partner and thus had elevated herself above the fray. No Black woman who sat through her confirmation hearings would have said she was above the fray. If I'm entirely honest, that was a bit of shared trauma that most of us did not want to experience in that moment, but we still wanted to support the moment and our sister (Morrison & Mascaro, 2022). Entirely too many of us could relate and it is why some of us are reluctant to head back to work in the office when we've been free of questions about our facial expressions thanks to Zoom's camera off feature (Onwuamaegbu, 2021). I'm sure you're wondering what this has to do with what I've been discussing. Well, let me tell you what I think ties it together. These women chose themselves over the prevailing narrative of who they should be and what they should accept in order to be happy. Doing that is one of the most radical forms of self-love and self-care available to Black women. Choosing our paths when the world keeps telling us that we cannot or should not do that is hard enough. Doing it and thriving is amazing.

That's the hope I have for Black women who share my story, understand my story, and/or are just beginning to walk into my story. Do what you do and continue to thrive. The work is draining and isolating sometimes. My mentor is an hour from me and we don't see each other as often as we could. Not because we don't want to but because we both have work to do on our campuses that doesn't always allow us to sit still and be silly together. When we do it's amazing and I want to be the next knitting psychologist but right now I just work on being more creative when we see each other at conferences. I've mentioned her before but let me recognize her brilliance again because it inspires me to keep pushing forward. Thank you, Dr. Sharon Bowman, for all you do and all you have given to the world writ large. The realization of how stressful the work is comes out when those of us who do it gather together. We are amazed at wins, share the grief of hesitation, and comfort those who are feeling defeated. It's a weird bit of lamentation and resetting that is needed if you are committed to trying to make the imperfect spaces we exist in better.

It can also be dangerous and scary sometimes. I had to watch a colleague I respect be attacked by right-wing media sources because she had the nerve to bring together a much-needed social justice conference for our university system (Kaminsky, 2021). The rest of us got nervous but she caught hell. And in the midst of that hell, she still pulled off an amazing conference that led me to another author in this collection. So let me pause here and recognize Dr. Monica Johnson for being her amazing self and making sure that the university didn't bow to hatred because we had that conference again the next year. I'm almost sure we'll be doing it again, so, yeah, the racists don't get to win no matter how much they try.

Ultimately, though, I hope the work turns out to be self-sustaining and time limited. Those replacements you will hear about later will need to step into the ranks at some point in the future because folks like myself, Drs. Johnson and Bowman, Judge Jackson, Serena, and the others will need to enjoy doing a bunch of nothing. I'm excited by the young doctors, athletes, lawyers, poets, artists, and others that seem poised to heed the call. They are passionate and most of all present. That's what the world needs to see most. The little Brown girls wanting to find their heroes and everyone else that needs to see that the future is filled with amazing, accomplished, and adept Black women ready to set the world on fire and burn down whatever refuses to work for everyone.

If you are not a little Brown girl or a not so little Brown girl reading this and you are wondering what to take from this, let me share the following. The Black women you know are likely some of your favorite people in the world. And if they have fed you, invited you over, or eaten your casserole, then please believe they love you, too. However, they are likely tired beyond measure right now. The few years prior to the pandemic were exhausting in ways that cannot be fully articulated. The pandemic exacerbated that stress. I have seen my colleagues leave fields and jobs we love because the stress of them is killing us without mercy. It's not always literal like in the case of Dr. Moore (Andone, 2020), but the workload, both compensated and free, is killing our spirits. Advocate for the Black women in your orbits. Make sure their hard work is routinely recognized. Do not just appreciate them when they are your sassy comic relief. Acknowledge when you may have made a mistake and challenge those around you to do the same. Most of all, though, it would be great for everyone involved if you could see them as a whole person and not just a caricature of Black womanhood. We come in a variety of iterations with a plethora of talents and foibles. Appreciate what we give to you and what would be missing from the world without us.

REFERENCES

Andone, D. (December 25, 2020). A Black doctor died of Covid-19 weeks after accusing hospital staff of racist treatment. CNN.com. www.cnn.com/2020/12/24/us/black-doctor-susan-moore-covid-19/index.html.

Bailey, M., & Trudy. (2018) On misogynoir: citation, erasure, and plagiarism. *Feminist Media Studies, 18*(4), 762–768. DOI: 10.1080/14680777.2018.1447395.

Bertrand, M., & Mullainathan, S. (2003). Are Emily and Greg more employable than Lakisha and Jamal? A field experiment on labor market discrimination. *National Bureau of Economic Research*, Working Paper 9873.

Gold, M., & Hennessey, K. (July 20, 2013). Michelle Obama's nutrition campaign comes with political pitfalls. *Los Angeles Times.* https://www.latimes.com/nation/la-na-michelle-food-20130712-story.html.

Hao, K. (December 4, 2020). "We read the paper that forced Timnit Gebru out of Google. Here's what it says." *Artificial Intelligence.* https://www.technologyreview.com/2020/12/04/1013294/google-ai-ethics-research-paper-forced-out-timnit-gebru/.

Kaminsky, G. (October 20, 2021). Indiana University spent 55K, sent publicly funded professors to promote critical race theory. *The Federalist.* thefederalist.com/2021/10/28/indiana-university-spent-55k-sent-publicly-funded-professors-to-promote-critical-race-theory/.

Kline, P., Rose, E. K., & Walters, C. R. (2021). Systemic discrimination among large U.S. employers. *National Bureau of Economic Research*, Working Paper 29053. www.nber.org/papers/w29053.

Levine, J. (May 14, 2022). Karine Jean-Pierre has frequent history of accusing things of being Racist. *New York Post.* nypost.com/2022/05/14/karine-jean-pierre-has-history-of-accusing-things-of-being-racist/.

Morrison, A., & Mascaro, L. (March 26, 2022). Black women feel sting of "traumatizing" Jackson hearings. *Associated Press News.* apnews.com/article/ketanji-brown-jackson-us-supreme-court-lifestyle-race-and-ethnicity-judiciary-39cda92bf12401ffeb0-b57f0d858adb3.

Oliphant, J. (February 26, 2011). Conservatives dig into Michelle Obama's anti-obesity campaign. *Los Angeles Times.* www.latimes.com/politics/la-xpm-2011-feb-26-la-na-michelle-obama-obesity-20110227-story.html.

Onwuamaegbu, N. (July 24, 2021). Many Black women felt relieved to work from home, free from microaggressions. Now they're told to come back. *The Washington Post.* www.washingtonpost.com/lifestyle/2021/07/24/black-women-office-work-home/.

Reuters Staff. (January 29, 2021). Fact check: Kamala Harris and Willie Brown had a relationship over a decade after he separated from wife. *Reuters.* www.reuters.com/article/uk-factcheck-kamala-harris-willie-brown/fact-check-kamala-harrisandwillie-brownhad-a-relationshipover-adecadeafterhe-separated-from-wife-idUSKBN26Y2RQ.

Shippie, A. T., & Debb, S. M. (2019). African American student achievement and the historically Black University: The role of student engagement. *Current Psychology, 38,* 1649–1661.

Chapter 3

We Don't Owe You a Smile

Jovan Shumpert

Dear white people,

In order for us to be able to discuss the violence that Black women face while working in white spaces, we must first give voice to the Black girls who enter predominately white educational institutions as children. These institutions are microcosms of the systemic racism we inevitably encounter as adults in the workplace. It happens early and often for Black women and is not something we can even avoid in our formative years.

EDUCATION

K–12 Years

My introduction to whiteness started early on. I grew up in St. Louis, Missouri, which is a city known for being among the most racially segregated in the country (Abello, 2019). Due to this racial segregation and socioeconomic inequity, schools in the Black and poor areas, similar to where I lived, suffered. School funding is based on local personal property taxes, which in turn determines one's access to quality education. As a way to combat these inequities, my parents along with many others opted to send their children to schools within white suburban school districts. "St. Louis's desegregation program, the longest-running and largest one in the nation, bussed over 70,000 inner-city black students to predominantly white schools in the suburbs" (Strauss, 2017). A program that continued through the 2010s, serving as an ongoing reminder of Black folks' subjugation, and how relevant the monumental the decision of *Brown vs. Board of Education* is to present day.

My initial introduction to a predominately white school district was positive. I remember my mother taking me to the school to meet the principal for a kindergarten screening before my official first day of school. We counted coins and played hopscotch in the hallway. I felt safe. The principal was a nice enough white man. As I matriculated, I made friends. Some Black, Asian, and white. I visited friends at their homes and attended birthday parties. It wasn't until third or fourth grade that I began to notice my place within society or at least at this micro level. I recall white people saying things like, "all Black people are poor" or "I thought all Black people lived in apartments." In response to a white girl mentioning that all Black people were poor, I used my *Black and scary card* and told her, "I'll whoop your ass." I didn't have the vocabulary or the knowledge that I have now to discuss how problematic her sentiments were, but I knew they were wrong, and I wanted to fight! A day or so later, my teacher called me outside of the classroom where I was met by my classmate and her mother. They demanded that I apologize for the threats that I had made, but no one ever contacted my mother about this incident or asked what warranted the threat. I was Black, and therefore the aggressor and guilty. Various racist acts took place throughout my childhood and adolescence. I call them racist acts as opposed to "microaggressions" due the prefix "micro," meaning small, in turn minimizing these behaviors.

By the time I reached sixth grade, I hated school. Most of the white friends that I had previously made were no longer friends. There was clear a divide. Many of the Black kids had been phased out of the desegregation program due to zoning efforts that prevented them from continuing to attend the district. I begged to be sent to a Black school. I knew that when the time came, I'd attend a Historically Black College or University (HBCU). I frankly needed a hiatus from white people. Luckily, at the time I met my first lifetime best friend, who was Black, equally as smart, and didn't take any mess. By seventh grade, we added another friend who also met the same qualifications, and another by eighth grade. During high school we had a wonderful principal with whom we all had a great relationship. He listened to our concerns and didn't shy away from discussing race. He was a white man from the South. He did not hesitate to tell us about the racist white men that we'd encounter in the South where most HBCUs are located. Unfortunately, he failed to mention the racist white women that we'd eventually work alongside and who are equally as vital to the maintenance of white supremacy (North, 2021). The Black women previously mentioned supported me throughout our tenure in the predominately white school district and continue to do so to this day. We all graduated and attended HBCUs.

College Years

Attending an HBCU is one of the best decisions that I have made in my life. Far from perfect, I felt safe. To see the look on my parents' and younger brother's faces when we arrived on campus for orientation is something that I will never forget. A Black utopia. An institution of higher learning For Us By Us (FUBU). An experience, I had never had. Although temporary, it was a place that protected us from the harms of racism, shaped our worldview, challenged us, and gave us the confidence to take on the world. North Carolina Agricultural and Technical State University became my Hilman College (Carsey et al., 1987–1993).

Graduate School

As a graduate student, I returned to my "Hilman" to receive a master's degree in clinical mental health counseling. The graduate program demographics differed from my undergraduate experience. The students ranged from traditionally aged students coming directly out of undergrad to people in their sixties and seventies, possibly working on a second or third career. I noticed more racial groups represented. The staff was majority Black, but there were also a few more white professors than I was used to having.

I had a positive rapport with most the staff, so much so that I found myself explaining to my white female professor that it is not appropriate to come to a class full of Black women and share her love for Madea (a fictional character in Tyler Perry's movies). My classmates and I sat in shock as this professor shared, "Madea is my Soul Sister. I love how she carries a gun in her purse and how her bosom sways from side to side."

Unbeknownst to our professor, Madea served as a "mammy" caricature, a racist stereotype. Mammy is typically an elderly Black woman who takes care of others while neglecting herself, lacks romantic interests, and is often overweight. One of the many caricatures found in the minstrel shows of the 1800s, where white people dressed up and "acted" as Black folks for their own entertainment. Only this time, Tyler Perry, a Black man, is in on the joke and has gained much notoriety and profit at the expense of Black women (Fontaine, 2011). It was a huge risk addressing these problematic statements within a professional setting with someone who held my future in her hands. It's a conversation that should have never happened.

RACISM IN THE MEDIA

Being victim to the crushing pressure of racism is not unique to me, unfortunately. More and more, Black women are sharing their trauma experienced in predominately white work spaces. Experiences that have led to them being pushed out of organizations, reprimanded, and sometimes even fired. We've watched this play out in very public ways. For example, witness Gabrielle Union losing her job with *America's Got Talent* after she brought forth concerns about "racism and sexism" creating a "toxic work environment" back in 2019 (BBC News, 2020).

We witnessed another instance of whiteness being wielded against Black women in March 2021 during the interaction between Sheryl Underwood and Sharon Osbourne on *The Talk*. Underwood questioned Sharon's public allegiance to Piers Morgan. Piers Morgan, a broadcaster on *Good Morning Britain*, who has notoriously targeted Meghan Markle, a bi-racial Black woman, who at that time was also Duchess of Sussex and wife of Prince Harry. No matter how warm Sheryl's approach was to Sharon, Sheryl Underwood was met with aggression, denial, demands to "teach me," and given the directive that she "better not cry" by her co-host and presumed "friend" Sharon Osbourne. The show was placed on hiatus due Sharon's racist actions, disrespect, and public outcry before her official exit from the show (Patten, 2021).

THE REAL WORLD

The story that I'll share is a story of problematic white women. A story that is still difficult to recall as I write about the topic of Black women in the workplace. I have worked for a number of employers prior to my return to the Midwest, specifically Indiana, but hadn't encountered racism to this degree. Experiencing covert racism is a gaslighting merry-go-round that convinces the target that they are the problem.

My previous employer was located in a rural, white, factory Midwestern town. I worked for a hospital network that has several contracts with local school districts and provided behavioral health services to the students within schools. Upon entry into the company, I originally worked in Indianapolis, Indiana. I did a two-hour commute to and from work during that time. After two years the commute became daunting, expensive, and time consuming. I lost a lot of free time and time spent with my daughter.

By early 2019, an opportunity was presented to me by a co-worker about a school-based therapy program being piloted where I lived. I applied and my application for transfer was approved. Shortly after my transfer was accepted, I met the new team and director. The director, a white woman, described the school district as a "Good ol' boys club." Myself and my then only Black co-worker darted eyes across the room to say, "did you just hear what I heard?" I rationalized, "well, I deal with racism in my current school, would this be any different?"

I accepted the position to assist with pioneering the new school-based team in the rural area that would place me fifteen minutes from home. During the first few weeks, I began to get to know my co-workers and met with administrators. We later walked around the school and met school staff. I can remember walking the halls and some would speak, while others would ignore attempts to be friendly. My white co-worker walked in a classroom ahead of me so we could introduce ourselves. As she brought her hand out to shake the teacher's hand, I began to follow up and do the same. The teacher began to extend his hand to my co-worker's hand, but as my hand came out he retracted his hand before reaching my co-worker's, then stated, "I just remembered, I'm sick." My response, "I appreciate you not sharing your germs."

Time went on, and I continued to meet teachers and began building relationships with students. Each school had a different culture. Some welcoming and happy to have us there, while others were colder. I was at the beck and call of each school and met their needs. I found myself having to bite my tongue to rude exchanges, to later being able to approach with tact.

Fast forward to August 2019, the first day of school. I received a phone call from my supervisor questioning me about the process of picking up a particular student that I worked with the previous semester. I shared that I went to the classroom, introduced myself to the teacher, asked if it was a good time, and shared how long I'd have the student. This was a typical process for pulling students out of the classroom. My supervisor stated that she had received an email from the school counselor, someone who was not happy about my team being there out of fear of job security and unhappy about my Black presence. The school counselor indicated concerns about my pulling the child of class with it being the first day of school and the teacher not knowing who I was. I left the phone call confused as to why I couldn't be told by school staff directly that there were concerns.

A week later, I made another attempt to get the same student, but this time during recess. I asked if it was a good time. The teacher said, "no" and seemed to be annoyed. I asked about other available times like lunch. I indicated that I would get her at lunch. I met with the student who enjoyed our lunch dates and went on about my day. I attempted to meet with the student the following week, but was told that she wasn't available.

In the weeks to follow, I ran into another challenge. I used an essential oil diffuser in a conference room that became a mobile office. The conference room had been housed within a suite shared with the school counselor, school secretary, and principal. I stayed in the room for four to five hours and wanted to provide a similar experience of my office. The next day, I came to work and found that I had a text message. The conversation is detailed in figures 3.1 and 3.2.

I continued my day as normal, yet uncomfortable in my work environment. We later had a departmental meeting and at the end I pulled my co-worker who texted me earlier aside. I told her that while I appreciated her efforts, I asked that she no longer speak on behalf of others. I also requested that she empower others to address me directly with any questions or concerns. She said OK, but her body language showed that she felt differently.

A few minutes after she left, she called me and had a little more to say. She shared that she didn't want to start anything and she thought it was best coming from her since we are co-workers. I assured her that my issue was with Karen and not her. I told her that I was still confused about why I was being

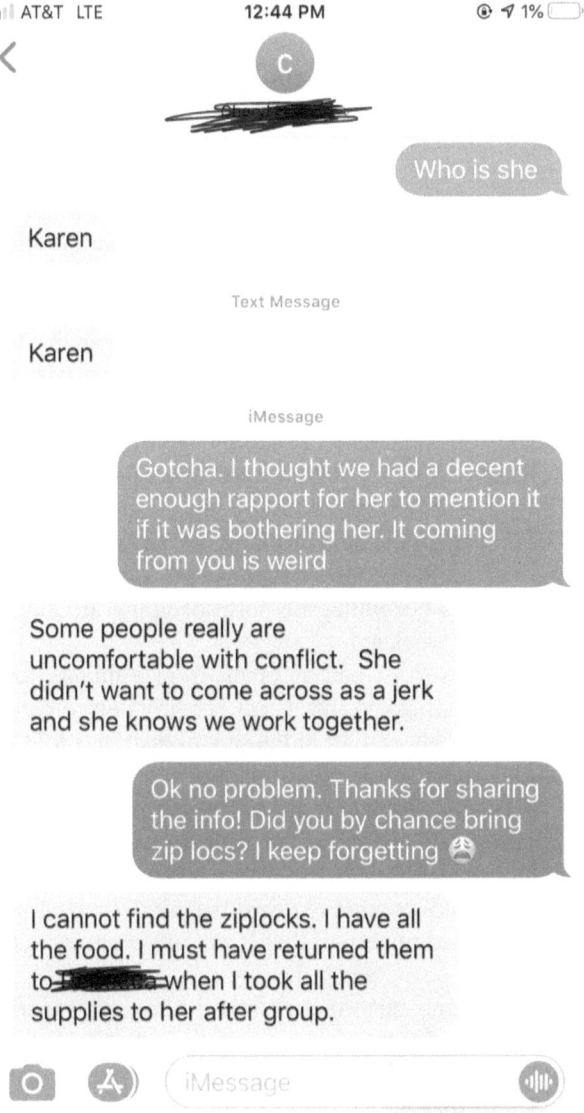

Figures 3.1 and 3.2. The Mission of White Supremacy Crumbles without the Complicity of White Women.
Source: Photos provided by author Jovan Shumpert.

fed information second hand. Then it happened! She told me that "there are some people at the school that think you're unapproachable." I remained calm and told her that it's hard to believe seeing that "I smile, speak upon entering rooms and do whatever it is being asked of me." She then added, "well if I'm being honest, I think you're unapproachable." I asked for examples of the ways that I had been unapproachable. Her answer: "well there's nothing you've said or done. I just feel like you're stand-offish. I feel like I have to walk on eggshells around you." I quickly learned that I had officially been deemed the Angry Black Woman (ABW). She attempted to make light and that we should have a closer relationship as co-workers. To close the conversation, I told her "it is not my job to make others comfortable. It is not my job to make others that are insecure with themselves comfortable around me."

After the conversation, I immediately went to our supervisor to express my concerns about me serving within this school district and the coded language being utilized to describe me as an Angry Black Woman. My supervisor apologized for my experiences and shared that she would talk with the director. She asked for what I needed as an employee. I reiterated the need for our diversity and inclusion director to come and give trainings, expressed the need for trainings and advocacy within the district. For accountability, I sent an email detailing my conversation with my supervisor to her and thanked her for listening. We met again the next morning for our weekly site visit and she assured me that she would encourage school staff to reach out to me directly as opposed to what was becoming the norm of going around me. This was right before Labor Day weekend.

Upon my return to work, I had an email from a human resources (HR) representative. The email asked that I call her privately. I called and I was immediately questioned about staff at the school district. I told her that I was confused and didn't know where all of this was coming from. She stated that allegations of racial discrimination are taken seriously and that the school district would have to do their own investigation. I provided information while also wanting to hold my co-worker accountable for her actions. The HR representative would eventually share that she received my email. My supervisor had forwarded my email that I sent after our conversation to HR without a word.

I later received a phone call from the school district's superintendent. He requested that we meet the following day. I agreed and reached out to HR and my supervisor to see if I needed any additional representation. The HR representative shared that the superintendent would be asking questions to hear my concerns for their investigation and that no one from HR would need to be present. On Wednesday, September 4, 2019, I met with the superintendent. The superintendent listened as I went through my three pages of written notes. He had even written his own notes and asked clarifying questions. He asked for ways that I could feel supported and was open to the idea of trainings. I also mentioned a recent posting that had been going around about one of his middle school teachers leading a "slave reenactment" in his social studies class. He assured me that one student uncomfortable is one too many and that the reenactment had been shut down. On Thursday, September 5, 2019, I was called to meet with my director. The meeting was odd in that I had never met with her on my own. I arrived in her office to see that there was another woman present. We were introduced and I was told that she would be an "unbiased" person. She continued, "we've received a 'third' email about you from the school." I was lost because I was not aware of a second and barely the first. She stated that she had gotten a number of complaints about me from teachers about picking students up from class. I had also been said to be rude and "unapproachable." Her tone was accusatory, condescending, and rude. I was then told that I was receiving corrective action, because I had been talked to several times. I asked about a verbal warning that hadn't been rendered. She replied that talks with my supervisor had been considered verbal warnings. I was then asked whether or not I would like to continue working in the school district. My response: "not if this would be my continued experience." She said that she would talk it over with her supervisor about my options and get back with me.

On Friday, September 6, 2019, I called HR to file a retaliation claim against my department. I met with a few students, but not many, because I was disengaged from the school district and clearly unwelcome. I was called back to the office that housed my supervisor, director, and my director's supervisor. I was told that I would be meeting with my director's supervisor. He greeted me with fake concern, sharing that he hadn't known much about me and that my performance appraisal was pretty good prior to my transfer. He stated that the past few weeks seemed to be hard for me. I agreed and shared what I thought he wanted to know, my experiences. Instead, he wanted to know what others had decided they knew about me, that I was an ABW. We discussed my options for work, and we decided that I would work with youth beginning that Monday in the outpatient office. I was asked, without warning, to report to the school, clear out my office, and report to the outpatient office.

As I cleared out my office, I felt numb. Relieved that I would no longer be in a school that was threatened by my very presence. Sad that I'd be leaving behind my clients due to no fault of my own. Angry that my company did not advocate for me knowing my work, my reputation, and the ways in which I helped pilot the program that they now made money from. On Tuesday, I called in sick and drove to Indianapolis to file a claim with the Employment Equal Opportunity Commission (EEOC) for Racial Discrimination and Retaliation. The following month I also reached out to employment lawyers. Unfortunately, because there hadn't been use of racial slurs, a firing, or a demotion, this type of covert harassment and racial discrimination would be difficult to prove. The best advice an employment lawyer gave me was to find a new job.

With the help of my community and my therapist, I remained employed with my then employer and began to develop an exit strategy. By October 2019, I took the licensure exam necessary to become a fully licensed therapist, which meant freedom. I was promised a salary increase, which I was entitled to due to my licensure status, but the amount quoted was blocked by my director. I worked with my therapist to take a much needed "stress" leave. I spoke with our benefits department, had appointments with my primary care physicians, and was eventually approved for a ninety-day paid leave. During the leave I began to create a wellness routine. I began going to yoga classes more frequently, continued attending therapy, tended to my plants, watched TV, read books, applied to jobs, prioritized sleep, and went on a long road trip to go visit some of my closest friends in the South. Lastly, I began to lay the foundation for my private therapy practice. I consulted with colleagues who were entrepreneurs, did research, obtained business mentors, and applied to the state to make my LLC a reality. By this time, COVID-19 rocked our collective worlds with more people discovering the importance of the mental health field. The timing was perfect.

Unfortunately, it takes time and money to build a private practice. I returned to work in April 2020, but luckily in a telehealth setting, and had the opportunity to work from home for a while. I felt safe and shielded from the expectations to constantly smile and make white people feel comfortable. I failed to mention that the director demanded that I "smile more" while issuing my write up months earlier. The case with the EEOC was eventually dropped. The harassment had slowed while the case was opened, but it soon returned with passive aggressive emails and comments about my work performance. I saved them all. By the summer, we were all back in the office full time, but with masks.

On August 25, 2020, I went to my interim supervisor's office to discuss ways that I could improve (to get the harassment to stop). I eventually broke down telling him everything. He sat in shock as I cried in his office. He apologized for my experience and shared that he had no idea, but he had figured something bad had happened with how quickly I transitioned from the school to the outpatient office. I then told him that I was tired of fighting and that I quit. I told him that I would finish whatever existing documentation that needed to be completed and would return the work laptop the following day. He asked if there was any other way he could get me to stay; I declined. I told the front office staff to cancel my appointments indefinitely, packed my office, and went straight to the emergency room to be seen as I had been experiencing chest pains consistently for weeks. Hospital staff reported that my blood pressure was elevated, gave me medicine for indigestion, monitored my heart, and eventually deduced that my chest pain was stress related. My director emailed me later that day asking for a formal resignation. I prepared a well thought out email that highlighted my experience as a Black woman within the company. I was sure to attach her harassing emails, my EEOC documentation, and my write up that included the word "unapproachable." The email was then sent to everyone that I could think of: heads of HR, the director's supervisor, my co-workers . . . everyone. I was finally free. Ultimately unemployed, but free.

REFERENCES

Abello, O. (2019, August 19). Breaking Through and Breaking Down the Delmar Divide in St. Louis. *Next City.* nextcity.org/features/breaking-through-and-breaking-down-the-delmar-divide-in-st.-louis.

BBC News. (2020, September 30). Gabrielle Union: America's Got Talent judge settles over show departure. *BBC News.* www.bbc.com/news/entertainment-arts-54353787#:%7E:text=Actress%20Gabrielle%20Union%20has%20reached,out%20against%20racism%20and%20sexism.

Carsey, M., Fales, S., Mandabach, C., & Werner, T. (Executive Producers.) (1987–1993). *A Different World.* [TV Series]. NBC.

Fontaine, N. (2011). From Mammy to Madea, and Examination of the Behaviors of Tyler Perry's Madea Character in Relation to the Mammy, Jezebel, and Sapphire Stereotypes." Thesis,

Georgia State University. https://scholarworks.gsu.edu/aas_theses/5.

North, A. (2021, January 15). White women's role in white supremacy, explained. *Vox.* www.vox.com/2021/1/15/22231079/capitol-riot-women-qanon-white-supremacy.

Patten, D. (2021, March 26). Sharon Osbourne Exits "The Talk" After Allegations Of Misconduct & Racist Remarks; Show Returns April 12. *Deadline.* https://deadline.com/2021/03/sharon-osbourne-exits-the-talk-controversy-cbs-piers-morgan-1234722968/.

Strauss, V. (2017, September 7). The sad story of public education in St. Louis. *The Washington Post.* www.washingtonpost.com/news/answer-sheet/wp/2017/09/07/the-sad-story-of-public-education-in-st-louis/.

Chapter 4

Find Your Replacements

Rosalyn D. Davis and Shantel Gaillard

From the moment I stepped into an academic setting, I have been privileged to some extent. Yes, I was a little brown girl surrounded largely by non-brown kids and teachers, but I had educated middle-class parents who wanted the best for me and who invested in my future. Because of that, despite the repeated frustrations that would come with being a smart Black girl, I had the energy and drive to keep trying to do my best. Even in those settings when I struggled, like in college because I was actually having to work and study for a change, I was lucky enough to have professors who listened to me. They heard my struggles and gave me advice on how to get to the next stage of my education or career. From Dr. Sheila Peters to Dr. Marcheta Evans and onto Dr. Sharon Bowman, I hit a trifecta of Black women with doctoral degrees in my chosen profession who could not only encourage me to keep on track but also serve as a role model for me.

My undergraduate institution was Fisk University, which to this day has a statue of Dr. W. E. B. Du Bois on campus. That matters because the whole mindset of the Talented Tenth both infused the campus and my experience as well as helped shaped the messaging I got from those women. For those who are unfamiliar with the Talented Tenth mindset, Du Bois (2014) opined that at any given point in time 10 percent of the Black population would be able to be educated. That 10 percent was responsible for going back into their communities and finding the next 10 percent to join the ranks. Now to be transparent, there are issues with that thought process and college is not a good fit for everyone. Not to mention after neighborhoods integrated, educated role models left the areas where the next 10 percent might be so there was a notable disconnect in what could have been and what actually took place. Had Du Bois understood mentoring from a less rigid viewpoint, or been more flexible in what could have been done, this concept may have been more successful.

My mentors didn't struggle with that as much. One said it explicitly and others intimated the same message. It was my job to find my replacements. To find the next generation of Black women in the helping professions whether they became psychologists or something else entirely. When I stepped out of a role, I needed to make sure that I had done what I could in order to make sure someone who looked like me or shared a similar experience was able to step into a position wherever she may be.

I began doing that as a graduate student and saw how excited former students were to get acceptances to graduate school after they worked with me on a project or received a letter of recommendation from me that helped complete their application. With each happy face, I shared the same directive—find your replacement. What you are going to read over the next few pages of this chapter is how one of my replacements has viewed that mentoring and what we have done together that will allow her to pursue whatever goals she has moving forward.

WORDS FROM THE FUTURE

My educational journey has been anything but predictable. I've often said, "I don't like school, but I love learning." I don't know if that's rooted in rebellion or independence. However, I have always known my purpose was in helping. My journey to where I currently sit—as a doctoral student in counseling psychology—was born from frustration, pain, and inspiration. My experience during my Peace Corps service in Jamaica, and an experience I had on a mission trip to Guyana, South America, solidified my decision to become a psychologist. My focus on public health had brought me to this point; however, I saw the need for individual-level work for my public health training had not prepared me for. At this point in my journey, I had never taken a psychology class and did not know any psychologists. I simply started doing internet searches and formulating a plan. I took my first psychology class at the local community college. I found it to be engaging and interesting, which solidified my decision to continue pursuing this direction. However, I had no idea what to do next. The community college didn't offer any other courses in psychology, so I made an appointment with the admissions office of the local university. I shared my past experiences and what I desired to do and the admissions officer (who happened to be working her last day before retirement) said, "You need to meet Dr. Davis, she will be able to help!" I met with Dr. Rosalyn Davis that same day and she hasn't been able to shake me since (not that she would want to!). I cried in that first meeting with Dr. Davis. I'm a focused, intelligent, driven Black woman, but there was a part of me that was afraid I wouldn't be able to bring this dream I was carrying to fruition. Failure had never been an option for me, but I was wondering if my dreams had surpassed my abilities. Dr. Davis had a quiet reassuring confidence, and I knew in that first meeting that I didn't have to figure this out alone. I'm still not sure what emotions those tears contained but I'm certain a portion of it was relief and hope.

I have been fortunate to have amazing Black women who have mentored me throughout my educational journey. Vicki Stewart Johnson, Jill Hill, Dr. Davis, and Dr. Sharon Bowman have each been sources of support, and have been confidants, advocates, and advisors. They have each broadened my understanding of what it means to be a mentor. My first experience with having a mentor was in the eighth grade. I was chosen to participate in a new program developed by the local university that targeted students transitioning to high school who had the potential to succeed in college but had an environmental factor that could be a barrier. I distinctly remember being confused about why I was chosen for this program. Yes, my parents were divorced but I had an amazing and supportive village composed of my large extended family and my religious community. Despite my personal perception of my clear path to success the research at the time suggested growing up in a divorced home was a risk factor to my educational attainment (McLanahan et al., 2013), more recent research has suggested differently (Brand et al., 2019). Regardless, in my mind attending college was always "when" and never "if"! As part of the program every student was matched with a mentor. So, in this instance, being a "statistic" was a blessing in disguise because it placed me in position to connect with Vickie. Having her as a mentor taught me the power of having someone (besides my family) to be fully vested in seeing me succeed. She demonstrated this by always showing up for me and not only being generous with her resources, but more importantly, her time. She started as a mentor and has become a lifelong friend. Mrs. Hill provided me my first research experience as a junior at Tuskegee University. It was summer, I felt like an adult, and I did not want to go home for the summer. I wanted to stay in my on-campus apartment and enjoy my independence. However, independence comes at a cost and I needed a job! I was desperate and feeling bold when I showed up at my dean's office (with no appointment) stating my case. He made a phone call (to his wife, I would later learn) and I had a student research position on a NASA-funded project! Mrs. Hill taught me the power and freedom of showing up as my most authentic unapologetic self and not being afraid of what I didn't know. I shared these earlier experiences because they provide context and understanding that I have had more than my fair share of amazing mentors. Yet, I have never experienced the type of all in, put you on my back and carry you (figuratively), you are going to execute your plan if we have to do daily check-ins (literally) mentorship that I have experienced with Dr. Davis and now Dr. Bowman. In a strange twist of fate or as I believe by divine design Dr. Bowman is now my doctoral chair. Being mentored by my mentor's mentor (that's a mouthful, huh?) is powerful—I know the ancestors are proud legacy building.

In reflecting on Dr. Davis's mentorship, I believe what has set her apart is that she is hands on. She not only demystifies the process, but she creates opportunities. All of my previous educational experience was related to biology and public health. When I needed research experience Dr. Davis simply said, "let's do a study." When I needed conference presentations, she reframed them simply as "discussions on whatever you want to talk about." By reframing all the barriers and requirements for advancement in this way, she transformed them into accessible learning opportunities for my continued growth and development. From that first meeting, Dr. Davis heard the plans that I had for myself and systematically helped me execute them. Every single time that I've felt lost or uncertain, she has shown up. Which has taught me that I can trust her, which is the foundation of the mentoring relationship (Chan, 2018). I've called, texted, emailed, and shown up in her office overwhelmed by the task at hand and been met with "what's going on, ma'am?" After each of these interactions, I've had what I needed to stay the course.

I have been actively mentoring young Black women since my days as an undergraduate at Tuskegee University. However, in the spirit of finding my replacement, and after experiencing the mentorship of Dr. Davis, I have a greater appreciation and a real understanding of what it actually means to be a mentor. Drawing from my own experience, mentors recognize talents and abilities that are not yet apparent to the mentee. They push the mentee beyond what they may think they are capable of, not allowing fear to stifle their growth. They provide encouragement when the mentee's faith is challenged and they create opportunities where none exist. Pfund et al. (2016) suggested positive mentoring experiences are the most important factor in completing a degree. Simply put, mentors are important and can literally make the difference between having a dream and living the dream.

AS LUCK WOULD HAVE IT

Mentoring is one of the ways in which access is granted to those who were excluded from the larger power structure (Mansfield, 2016; Pahkale, 2021). If we are lucky, we have mentors who have been able to achieve what we are seeking in our own lives and can share their roadmaps with us. If we are very lucky, they will expand that process to include others in their network so that we have a tether across a profession or area of the country. If we are blessed, we exist long enough to take that effort and expand it to others who we meet and who will one day replace us. I will touch on each of those aspects of mentoring along with one other. What happens when we are unlucky across the board? That is a different experience and one that can be demoralizing and lead to damaging behavior being experienced and inflicted on others.

If you have seen the musical *Guys and Dolls*, then you have likely heard "Luck Be a Lady Tonight" at some point in your life. You may not remember the lyrics but essentially the crooner is asking that luck be on their side tonight and not derail their efforts. Being a young professional Black woman can feel much like that if you are not from a long line of people who know the path you plan to walk on. I mentioned my own bouts with luck, but what I skipped over was, while I found my home in psychology, my original path in college was a different field entirely. I went to college to deliver babies in the future. I liked science, and my parents wanted a doctor in the family, so yeah, let's do that. Except, I hated large chunks of what I was studying. There were plenty of Black women to guide me there and this is a not a knock on them at all. They were the most encouraging group of women, save one, I could have hoped for and told me that I may have to work harder on the things I didn't enjoy but that I could do the work if I wanted to do so. What I wish one would have said is that I could have been helpful, or a doctor, in something I completely enjoyed instead of suffering through because that's what Black women are expected to do. When I finally was forced to make a decision in order to remain in college, I did switch my major and found a freedom in psychology that did not exist in biology. It would be later that I fully understood the racism and sexism embedded in the field but for the next year and a half I was in heaven. When you finally have your place after feeling out of sorts, it can be intoxicating and I honestly didn't want to leave. However, Dr. Peters was very clear about two things. First my undergraduate GPA was looking a little bruised because of my insistence on delivering babies. Second, she wasn't sure that my HBCU could deliver the kind of graduate education I would need to be competitive in the long run. It took a lot of honesty to have both conversations, but I needed to hear them and adjust accordingly. I stayed in town very briefly after graduation to hear from a few of the employers I had applied to, but after hearing nothing I went home and regrouped. This may sound like a devastating development, but honestly I don't know how much time I would have wasted without that intervention. At least I was heading home with a degree in hand and the ability to reach out again. Luck was on my side.

I planned for a gap year, but the real-world employment situation was not amazing and I only spent a semester out of school. I continued my lazy habit of only applying to a limited number of graduate programs but was admitted to both programs. One was near where I had done my undergraduate work and let me know two weeks before classes started, while the other was local but admitted me on probation because, while my grades were middling, my

GRE scores were strong. I should pause here and reveal another bit of luck from that time in undergrad. As I was preparing for graduation, someone in the financial aid office asked me if I was taking any of the graduate school entrance exams. I said no because I hadn't even considered such exams existed. Yes, I had taken the SAT and ACT to get into college, but the counselors stayed on top of us to do those things. No one was asking us about the MCAT, LSAT, or GRE if we weren't asked about it ourselves. She told me to reconsider because my EFC on my FAFSA was zero so I qualified to take the GRE for free. She had just processed the waiver form for someone else. It helps to go to a small school, I promise. So I said okay and we filled out the paperwork to take both the general exam and psychology subject test for free. Those scores, in combination with my GPA, allowed me to at least be considered for graduate work. As I said before, luck was on my side.

I was not in a place financially or emotionally to head back to my former place of residence so I stayed home and went to the program that put me on probation. You have to know me to know that I saw that as an insult and a challenge. I had to hit at least a 3.0 GPA at the end of the first semester or I wouldn't be allowed to continue. What neither the program nor I knew at the time was I loved graduate-level work. Whereas undergraduate education normally commits to making you a well-rounded person, graduate education provides you with expertise in a specific subject. That means limited to no courses that do not directly relate to making you a better future professional. I did well in my undergraduate psychology courses, but I crushed my master's program. The first and only B I got in my master's program came that initial semester and I finished it with a 3.66 GPA. After that, I was granted a graduate assistantship that paid for my courses, paid me a stipend, and gave me training experience that I would not have received otherwise. I was a grader for multiple semesters, worked in our mock training studio, helped professors with research, and was coerced into my first publication by a professor who knew I was one of the GAs. It was a tongue-in-cheek paper about the lack of social life one has as a graduate student and ways to cope that wouldn't add to the low level of depression one may have throughout the program.

I also connected to Dr. Marcheta Evans through that work and watched her do amazing things in the same way that I had watched Dr. Peters previously. I was able to seek out Dr. Evans's counsel after several professors said I should at least consider applying to doctoral programs and what that work would look like in case I chose to pursue it. She shared advice that I pass on as well now, if I didn't want to teach then there may not be a benefit to me getting it in the long run but that it wasn't bad to have because there were more options open to me. My graduate assistant group was also by and large applying to doctoral programs. I had no desire to be the weak link of the collective and thought we had all had similar experiences so if they qualified I would too.

Honestly, I wasn't aware of how competitive doctoral programs were because I likely would not have applied. What I did know was my professors had prepared me well and their pathway to success had been shared with me so I did what they did. That included serving as a student volunteer at a professional psychology conference. That volunteer work allowed me to interview with one of my potential doctoral homes and decide without the expense of travel that we were not a match. While it eliminated one of my three choices, I had interviews with three of the four programs I had applied to, it also made me hyperaware of what I was looking for in a training program after seeing how disinterested these professors seemed to be in their students. So, luck abounded in my master's program but it was going to explode on the next step of my journey.

Let me just say that while I was probably the luckiest mentee on the planet to have a Black female professor available to me at each stage of my educational journey, I was entirely unaware of how uncommon that was as I was experiencing it (Mansfield, 2016). Meeting Dr. Sharon Bowman during my interview with the doctoral faculty was for me pretty normal. Here was another phenomenal Black woman that could be my guide should I be admitted. Like Dr. Peters, she was doing research, serving on external boards, and a known entity in the community. Like Dr. Evans she was mentoring students and in a position of leadership. Unlike both of them though, Dr. Bowman was literally queen of the proverbial mountain. The interview day was stressful. There were professors who I was sure I wanted to avoid if I was admitted. However, I knew more than anything when I left that visit that I wanted to be in that program because I needed to learn from Dr. Bowman how to lead without letting it block your energy and your ability to thrive among a litany of other things. I was just a little crestfallen when I was initially waitlisted for the program because I thought I had crushed the interview. Remember, I had no idea at all how competitive this process was and that even being waitlisted for a ten-person cohort was better than the alternative. Thankfully, someone had the desire to be somewhere else and I was admitted to the program. Yes, I learned a lot and was able to do all of the things that I know got me my first professional position. And yes, I had other professors who were immensely supportive and allowed me to grow under their guidance. However, every luck-granting deity was tinkering in my future when Dr. Bowman agreed to be my committee chair.

This is where we got into the work of being a Black female psychologist. I learned all the skills and techniques, but I also learned how to navigate working with people who weren't sure what to do with me in clinical and professional settings. I was taught how to do research that was important to me and to those that looked like us and how to do it with a student who didn't see themselves as gifted as those she was working with. I was not told to make myself small or diminish my intelligence, but I was taught how to assess rooms for how to use all of my skills to my benefit and to convince others that they wanted to be connected to all of those skills. I learned the value in not reacting in spaces where people were hoping to disparage you and your abilities as well as the thing that sits with me most to this day. Because I had been gifted with all of these new educational targets that were extracurricular to my actual education, I had another task. Much in the way that Dr. Bowman had guided me along the way over the short course of four years, I needed to do the same thing for the young Black women who would come to me because of my roles. To say that I didn't see myself on any level with my previous mentors was an understatement. However, it's not always what we see in ourselves but what others see in us along the way that matters more.

My first unofficial research assistant was a young Black woman who was considering pursuing a master's degree in counseling. She had questions about the process and the benefits of the field, and I needed someone who still liked going to the library and didn't get a massive headache combing through microfilm. Yes, ladies, gentlemen, two spirit and nonbinary friends, I am microfilm old. We met sporadically over the course of a semester and our exchange of labor ended up netting me twenty articles I didn't have to fetch and print while she received a glowing letter of recommendation. She was a great student who had gone above and beyond anything related to the course she had with me, so it was not a hard letter to write. She was the first of my network to go off to graduate school and succeed. She wasn't the last and I am grateful for that. Luck has allowed me to watch my network grow to include students across gender and racial lines even though the vast majority are minoritized on some level (race, ethnicity, sexuality, immigration status, and so on) and the largest segment are Black women. My co-author on this chapter is one of them and I am grateful that I have been able to remain present in the field for the last two decades and scatter that energy and influence across multiple states and settings.

I have mentored students through professional organizations, work settings, and who come to me after they see me present and want to follow up on something I have shared with them there. Some of these relationships are deliberate because I want to be part of supporting a specific kind of student or young professional. Others are more fluid and happen completely by happenstance. Overall, it's a unique position to be in to watch yourself become one of the people that your younger self would have pestered for guidance. It's an amazing moment though to watch your mentees grow and develop and embrace the knowledge you are passing on and passionate about sharing. At some point, all of the women I look up to will retire and I will be sad about that. However, I know that just as they poured into me they have poured into others so those Black women and men, those POC, those allies that they have taken under their wings will be there to fill in the gap and share their well-earned knowledge on to the next generation of scholars. I am luckier still that my mentees have embraced the two pieces of advice I give to everyone who asks before we target their individual needs: to find their replacements and to make people tell you no when you ask for things. Embracing those messages has given me access to experiences and opportunities that would not have been available if I just assumed that I wasn't qualified, knowledgeable enough, or ready to take on a challenge. And I have watched it play out with a nervous mentee hoping that they are allowed access to the next big task they want to pursue. If you do get a no, then it was not time for that particular thing to come to fruition. However, it's amazing how many times the answer is yes and all you needed to do was ask or apply.

So as you are sitting here now thinking about who you may want to reach out to in order to help guide yourself forward, don't wait too long or you may miss your opportunity. The only real downside to always looking for your replacements is the number of people who need your help and the illegality of human cloning. Okay so that last part is a joke but the first is not. I am trying to finish a research project now that will involve me working with my chapter co-author and an Asian male student who has had the temerity to ask for the opportunity. That's great for me and them because the project will be completed. However, that means that others who are just mustering the courage to ask now will not have room on this project and until it is completed will have to wait in the wings.

If you are reading this and thinking about the number of people who are needing your guidance, it's okay to acknowledge that you don't have the bandwidth for the next project or another mentee. Bad mentoring is almost worse than no mentoring. We have to take care of ourselves otherwise they will be replacing us faster than they should. I have appreciated when Dr. Bowman has told me that she cannot complete a project with me or respond to something quickly. It reminds me to slow down and be still as well. All of this is part of my abundance of blessings.

I do want to share a brief aside about bad mentoring. We are not immune to failure in the mentoring process. I have had a few mentees who opted to make decisions that I believed would likely not be to their benefit but couldn't find a good way to say that without hurting their feelings. I may have also taken on mentees because they looked like me that I should have given to someone else because we didn't connect in a way that my support was always present and untethered to any expectations. I know that is problematic because those kinds of issues haven't worked well for me when I have experienced them as a mentee. The relationship between mentor and mentee only works to the extent that both people want to be in the relationship and are able to connect over time. You've heard about mentors who greatly influenced me but for the sake of everyone involved I will not identify those who were not as successful. I will say that it is good to know how each person works and to respect that when possible. I am someone who is always very direct and who attempts to be as clear as possible when we communicate. That means that I do not enjoy interacting with people who equivocate a lot and who are focused on maintaining superficial relationships. I am also someone who adheres to deadlines as much as possible so if something is due on the twelfth of the month, I will likely give it to you at least a day early if possible. If not, you'll get it as close to the twelfth as possible with apologies if it is late. Mentoring relationships for me that have short-circuited usually have had delays in communication as well. Finally, we also have to recognize that not everyone is meant to be or skilled as a mentor. It requires some emotional heavy lifting sometimes and it requires some dedication and focus. If we cannot do those things or do not possess those skills, we may be doing our mentees a disservice.

So, let's try to wrap this up on a more positive note. Mentoring can be an amazing gift to both mentor and mentee. As I watch each of my mentees grow, I get to celebrate their accomplishments and their development as they become fixtures in the field. Their excitement and realizations keep me invested in the work that I do and have been lucky enough to do for the last twenty years. Having a mentee develop a chapter with me was more fun than I could have imagined it would be when we talked through what she wanted to do. And while she gave me credit for all of those opportunities she was able to pursue, the fact of the matter is she met each challenge and ran with it. I may give you the project but after that I want to see what you do with it. My joy comes from watching their spark and self-belief come to the fore. That moment when they see themselves in the way that I have seen them for quite some time. Those moments will never grow old even if I do and there are more memories to hold than my jumbled up office can contain.

The act of mentoring also allows me to reconnect to my mentors along the way and thank them for their willingness to listen to and support a formerly naïve but incredibly motivated young Black woman who had finally found her home. Without them, there would be no me and this book would have never been an idea let alone a finished product. They watched me in the same way I watch my mentees. They watched me go from nervous seeker to confident producer and loud advocate. The perspective is amazing when you are able to be present long enough for the process to come full circle. So pay more attention to the quiet ones in your classrooms. They may just need someone to amplify their voice (Pahkale, 2021). Spend time actively explaining office hours and inviting students to stop by. You may just inspire someone to seek their own pathway and try to capture the wonder they used to have when they thought about their future. Talk to the tired colleague, the single mom, the anxious athlete (Pahkale, 2021). Any of them could be the reason you are smiling brightly on a random Wednesday when you finish reading your email for the day. Find your replacements, dear readers, and I hope that luck is always on your side.

REFERENCES

Brand, J. E., Moore, R., Song, X., & Xie, Y. (2019). Why does parental divorce lower Children's educational attainment? A causal mediation analysis. *Sociological science, 6*, 264–292.

Chan, A. (2018). Trust-building in the mentoring of students of color. *Mentoring & Tutoring: Partnership in Learning, 26*(1), 4–29.

Du Bois, W. E. B. (2014). *The problem of the color line at the turn of the twentieth century: The essential early essays.* Fordham University Press.

Mansfield, K. C. (2016). *Identity intersectionalities, mentoring, and work–life (im)balance: Educators (re)negotiate the personal, professional, and political.* Information Age Publishing.

McLanahan, S., Tach, L., & Schneider, D. (2013). The causal effects of father absence. *Annual Review of Sociology, 39*, 399–427. doi.org/10.1146/annurev-soc-071312-145704.

Pahkale, S. (2021). Mentoring minorities: Five foundational lessons. *The American Journal of Medicine, 134*(10), 1300–1303.

Pfund, C., Byars-Winston, A., Branchaw, J., Hurtado, S., & Eagan, K. (2016). Defining attributes and metrics of effective research mentoring relationships. *AIDS and Behavior, 20*(2), 238–248. doi.org/10.1007/s10461-016-1384-z.

Chapter 5

I Need No Qualifiers

Vanessa Costello-Harris

Du Bois's (1903) book, *The Souls of Black Folks*, discussed the double-consciousness experienced by Blacks in America, stating that:

> After the Egyptian and Indian, the Greek and Roman, the Teuton and Mongolian, the Negro is a sort of seventh son, born with a veil, and gifted with the second-sight in this American World,—a world which yields him no true self-consciousness, but only lets him see himself through the revelation of the other world. It is a peculiar sensation, this double-consciousness, this sense of always looking at one's self through the eyes of others, of measuring one's soul by the tape of a world that looks on in amused contempt and pity. One ever feels his two-ness,—an American, a Negro; two souls, two thoughts, two unreconciled strivings; two warring ideals in one dark body, whose dogged strength alone keeps it from being torn asunder. (p. 2)

Like many Black women I can't help but see myself through the reflection of society's eyes. A reflection fueled by stereotypes that have crossed generations; the uneducated Black woman raised in the ghetto, the angry Black woman, the strong Black woman, and the promiscuous Jezebel (Thomas, Hacker, & Hoxha, 2011). I look in the mirror and see two people; I see who I am and who society assumes I am. I acknowledge the lens of society's stereotypes and move through my day accordingly. I push forward determined to not allow these stereotypes to hinder my progress, impact my education or diminish my accomplishments.

As of 2020 approximately 15% of students enrolled in secondary education identified as Black/African American compared to 50% who identified as non-Hispanic White (US Census Bureau, 2021). Similar demographic trends are observed in postsecondary education with Blacks and non-Hispanic Whites accounting for 15% and 50%, respectively, of the student population.

With these demographics it should come as no surprise that I was educated in predominately White spaces. I'm originally from Southern California and the youngest of three children raised in a single-parent household. I grew up around family—aunts, uncles, cousins—and had multiple examples of Black success. My formal education began at the age of four and was always made a priority. I went to predominantly White schools from preschool through graduate school with most of my teachers, friends, and peers identifying as White. I was placed in the Gifted and Talented Education program (GATE) early in my education and always knew I was receiving more advanced coursework than other students outside of my class. Historically, ethnic minority students have lower access to and participation in programs like GATE. For example, as of 2014, schools offering GATE or similar programs reported campus demographic's consisting of 49% White students and 42% Black and Latino students. Yet, a greater proportion of White students (57%) versus Black and Latino students (28%) were placed in GATE (US Department of Education, 2016).

I was typically the only Black child in my class and part of the only Black family in my neighborhood, something that was viewed as a matter of fact versus a topic of concern. As a child I rarely thought about my Blackness or how it caused the world to perceive or treat me differently. It's not that I was "color-blind," the token term to suggest that one's behavior toward others is not influenced by their perceived race or ethnicity (Holoien & Shelton, 2012), I knew I was different and treated differently than my peers even without fully understanding why. I spent years hit with questions about why I didn't wear sunblock (a mistake I've corrected as an adult), why I had burn marks on my ears from a hot comb (then explaining what a hot comb was), why I didn't wash my hair every day, and how I was able to magically take a shower without getting my hair wet. Yes, I was different, but it took time for me to explicitly consider how these differences could negatively impact me. I was blissfully unaware of the *veil*. Unaware of the social factors that separated me from my friends. I began to feel the presence of the veil by adolescence that paralleled my explicit exposure to prejudice views from others. "Nigga," a word commonly heard in music and at family functions—growing up the word didn't faze me, being called a nigga didn't affect me but being called a "Nigger" was like a splash of ice water on an already cold day. In adolescence I remember the hurt I felt when my friends told me our new neighbors called them "nigger lovers" and I felt betrayed when these friends continued to hang around them. More than once, the mother of a close friend referred to me as her daughter, yet she once compared Blacks and Whites dating like zebras and horses. We are similar but not the same. After those, and similar experiences, I would always wonder if those I interacted with truly saw me as the same as them or just similar. If I'm only similar, then was I viewed as less than? Would my abilities and accomplishments be viewed as less than? Would the expectations people hold for me be lower or assignments graded easier because of others already expecting less from me and me exceeding those low expectations? I've always been told I was smart for a Black person. That was one of my first back-handed compliments that confirmed my suspicion of my "less than" status.

BACK-HANDED COMPLIMENTS

Back-handed compliments leave you feeling flattered with a bad taste in your mouth. Like newly spoiled milk, refreshing until you realize the aftertaste might make you vomit. I never understood why some people would end their compliments of my beauty, intelligence, demeanor with "for a Black person." I was "pretty for a Black person, smart for a Black person, well-spoken for a Black person," and in college I had an explicit racist tell me I was "pretty cool for a Black person." I now know back-handed compliments for what they truly are: microaggressions. Racial microaggressions have been defined as "brief and commonplace daily verbal, behavioral, or environmental indignities, whether intentional or unintentional, that communicate hostile, derogatory, or negative racial slights and insults toward people of color" (Sue et al., 2000, p. 271). Intentional or not, all these "compliments" with qualifiers were just sweet words tainted with prejudice. Adding this qualifier contributed to me questioning my own Blackness. If I was smart, well-spoken, or attractive for a Black person, does that mean I'm failing in what society views as "being Black"? Was I the "Oreo" or "Uncle Tom" people joked about? Was I not Black enough? Did I have the right to attend Black Student Union meetings, be offended by racial comments, or express pride in Black accomplishments? Adding these qualifiers also reduced my accomplishments, as if my beauty, intelligence, or skills could only be viewed as exceptional if the comparison was being made to other Black individuals; Black individuals who must be viewed as less than their White counterparts.

Black students at predominately White institutions report microaggressions related to lower academic expectations from peers and faculty (Solórzano, Ceja, & Yosso, 2000). Awareness of lower expectations results in students questioning their own academic abilities and working harder to not confirm stereotypes. Before college I rarely feared people questioning my academic abilities due to my racial status, a luxury I attribute to my brother. My brother is a year older than me and always excelled academically. He participated in GATE, enrolled in honors classes, and participated in college preparatory courses. I followed suit and teachers expected me to excel as he did. If anything, I was more afraid of being judged for my gender versus race. My brother wasn't granted the same luxury and moved through his early academics questioning his skills and worked hard to overcome perceived racial scrutiny. These experiences drove his decision to leave predominately White spaces and attend Morehouse College, a Historically Black College (HBCU).

I didn't grow up with knowledge of HBCUs and only became aware of them when my brother attended Morehouse during my senior year of high school. I relished the idea of being independent in another state, meeting more people like me, and knowing that if I stood out, it would be purely due to my skills and not influenced by my race. Socially and academically people would recognize me because my skills would make me memorable versus my melanin. No longer would I question if the explicit compliments I was provided were quietly followed with the "for a Black person" qualifier. Spelman College seemed to be my next step. For the first time I would be surrounded by Black excellence beyond the boundaries of my family. I remember visiting the college, meeting up with my brother, and thinking, "I can't move across the country to live next door to my older brother, once again blocked by his shadow." I missed the application deadline.

Over the years I've wondered if I gave up too quickly. Why did I not consider searching for other HBCUs and why was it so easy for me to not push harder to transcend into predominantly brown spaces? In the end I enrolled at California State University, Fullerton, and was yet another brown face in a predominately White space. During my sophomore year I had three major experiences that influenced me. I attended my first Afro-Studies class, had my first Black professor, and attended a class where most of the students were Black. For the first time in my academic experience, I was able to hear about Black history without the weight of discomfort projected by other students when discussing slavery or the Civil Rights Movement. For once I didn't feel the weight of responsibility to provide life examples of present-day discrimination. I was exposed to Black pains from the past and more importantly was shown an abundance of evidence of Black success. I left most classes feeling empowered and validated that my family was not the exception to the rule; Black success had radiated through the centuries, it just wasn't being taught within mainstream education.

I hate that I spent so much of my adolescence questioning what those statements meant, " . . . for a Black person." I was just as smart and spoke just as well as everyone else in my family. Even today, within my immediate and extended family I have the most degrees, the highest degree, and have spent the greatest amount of time in academic environments. By most standards the average person would view me as a success without the qualifier and a Black unicorn with it. Yet I can honestly and humbly say when comparing myself to others in my family I am not the smartest person, most well spoken, the best writer, the strongest public speaker, the best at math, the most artistic, or most musically inclined. Within my family I am not the exception to the rule, I'm the continuation of it. Afro 101 provided me with evidence of what I knew all along, I was not "smart for a Black person" or "successful for a Black person." I am smart, I am Black, and I am successful, period. My success needs no qualifiers nor will my Black identity be reduced to help others feel comfortable with my accomplishments.

STEREOTYPE THREAT: MAINTAIN YOUR OWN STANDARDS AND BE PREPARED FOR OPPORTUNITIES

Growing up I experienced high levels of stereotype threat; living in fear of confirming stereotypes or even worse, fear of realizing the stereotypes people held about me were true (Steele & Aronson, 1995). I cognitively reframed my challenges as time for learning and improvement; I ignored the explanations society provided. For example, when I struggled at math and science, I reminded myself that my gender and race had nothing to do with it, the material just hadn't "clicked" yet. When a faculty member used words and I had no idea of the meaning; I reminded myself I wasn't less educated for not knowing but had a career path that exposed me to different vocabulary. Nonetheless, my reframing didn't equate to the reframing of others. I refused to let their negative assumptions about any of my group identities influence who I became.

I wasn't just impacted by racial stereotypes but stereotypes and statistics of being young, female, lower socioeconomic status, and raised in a single-parent household. Television shows, the news, daily interactions in town: they were constant reminders of the perceived shortcomings of the different groups I belonged to. I've experienced racism for being Black, sexism for being female, and usually a frustrating combination of the two for being a Black female. Crenshaw (1989) discussed the intersectionality of Black women who are multiply burdened with their membership to two marginalized groups (being Black and being female), with the intersection of the group membership resulting in greater burden than having singular membership. My experience is not just that of a Black individual but as a young Black female. In college I realized I could fail and disappoint my family but for the rest of society I would just be confirming what they already believed; my chances of success, my chances of overcoming obstacles were slim. I considered the risk of just being average, of just doing the minimum; why push myself beyond what others expected of me, what was the point? I was faced with the realization that I could build up or burn down my future. I became angry, angry at the fact that I had the option, angry that the world didn't hold greater expectations for me and determined that I would not conform to these stereotypes. I would not let history or societal beliefs define me or what I did moving forward. I carried this mentality through college and was determined to set my own standards and goals based on what was important to me.

I began my undergraduate experience as a psychology major with a goal of becoming a mental health therapist. While my goal was set, I had no idea of the requirements necessary to achieve it. Each semester I went to my academic advisor, pulled out my checklist of completed classes, and watched my advisor check a dozen boxes. No career goals nor areas of interest were ever discussed. Yet, with each necessary box checked, I believed I was on my way to reaching my goals. If at any point I began to drift astray my academic advisor would stop me from drifting too far off course. I realize now that I did not need an academic advisor who checked boxes. I needed an academic mentor, someone who knew what would be required to achieve my career goals and how that would translate to my academic preparation. I needed someone who could give me alternative options within my area of interests and field of study. At the start of my sophomore year I decided that becoming a mental health therapist was not the path for me. While 33% of college students change their major at least once before graduation (Leu, 2017), I didn't have the same luxury. Being a low-income student, I couldn't afford to enroll in extra courses or complete unpaid internships to explore my career options. By the end of my first year I could already see my financial aid dwindling and student loans growing. White students' odds of graduating with an associate's or bachelor's degree within five years of starting college are 43% higher than Black students' (Ross et al., 2012). For me, requiring more than four years to graduate was not a financial option. At the time I was working for a company that provided services to children, teens, and adults with disabilities. I enjoyed my work but hadn't considered how a psychology degree would allow me to create a career from my current experiences and interests. How could I prepare for a career without having a career in mind? The best I could do was be prepared for various opportunities that might come my way.

Preparation meant raising and maintaining my own standards with the belief that, when opportunities presented themselves, I would be ready and qualified for what came my way. I've been described as ambitious, a perfectionist, and an over-achiever; none of which I believe to be true. My accomplishments aren't due to some deep desire to be the best, to show excellence, or be a walking example of success. I've learned the importance of being prepared to identify and accept opportunities that allow me to better myself, my situation, and others around me. Such an opportunity occurred during my second year in college. I was taking a psychology course in child and adolescent development. I sat in the front rows, paid attention in class, and volunteered answers during class discussions. I didn't do anything special; I did what was expected. One day the professor spoke with me after class and questioned me on my academic progress and future goals. She provided me details of a research program that prepared participants for PhD-level graduate programs. The program was geared towards increasing diversity (e.g., ethnic, socioeconomic status, gender, etc.) in biomedical fields of study. If I was accepted, I would have the opportunity to work one-on-one in the research laboratory of a PhD-level faculty member, obtain two years of tuition coverage, be a paid research assistant, and provided funds to travel and present at research conferences across the country. I was facing a fork in the road with both paths riddled with uncertainty and opportunities for failure and success.

Years later I've come to view this moment as a pivotal point, both personally and professionally. One side was my current path: unsure of my career options, continued meetings with my advisor checking boxes, growing debt, and me obtaining a psychology degree with minimal ideas of what I could and would want to use it for. The only barriers to my success would be not passing my classes. The other side was acceptance to the program: greater financial security, enhanced coursework, less flexibility in selecting my courses, personal interactions with professional women in the field, and creating a set of circumstances that would require me to raise expectations for myself and placing myself in situations where I would be considered average at best. Potential barriers to success: I knew very little about research, I hated the one research course I completed, and couldn't envision what my life would look like if I committed to a more academic path.

I'm a first-generation student who grew up with the expectation that I would complete a four-year degree. My family always emphasized the importance of education and supported my academic choices but being one of the first to complete a four-year degree meant I had limited guidance in my academic decisions. However, I did have guidance in my financial decisions and, financially, applying for the research program was the best choice. I was accepted into the Minority Access to Research Careers (MARC; now known as Maximizing Access to Research Careers) program and was suddenly transformed from "Vanessa the psychology major at a school of 30+ thousand students," to "Vanessa, MARC Scholar." I didn't feel like a scholar; I looked at my MARC peers and saw scholars in training while I felt like a novice playing catch-up. I suddenly had professional cards, keys to campus laboratories, my own office space, and a title; but I lacked the knowledge and skills to view myself as an academic equal to my MARC peers. I was in a multidisciplinary program and exposed to research within psychology, chemistry, biology, and computer science. The first article we were assigned was a four-page paper on apoptosis (cell death) that took me four days to decipher enough to read and even longer to comprehend. I spent hours highlighting words I didn't know, looking up definitions, and rewriting sentences with terms I could easily understand. I rewrote sections in my own words, then explained and discussed the articles with my friends and family. I was struggling to be average in this new realm of excellence, but when I looked in the mirror I saw a MARC Scholar. I was determined to push myself until I felt like my reflection looked in the mirror.

"Fake it 'till you make it," and hope you don't feel like an impostor along the way. Imposter syndrome is defined as a feeling or self-belief that one is not as intelligent or skilled as their performance would indicate and one day everyone will discover their imposter status (Clance & Imes, 1978). I'd be lying if I said there weren't times that I felt like an impostor, like me being accepted into these spaces of excellence were somehow due to me sneaking under the bar. Yet, my imposter feelings weren't chronic, they were brief moments in time when I wondered, "What the hell have I gotten myself into and who let me do it? Am I really qualified to be in this space, do others around me believe the same thing, and am I hurting the future chances of others like me from earning similar opportunities?" In the beginning, research conferences were the places I experienced the worst of both worlds, due to my heightened awareness of my young Black female status in these predominately White spaces. Despite my weekly interactions with two female scientists, my mental prototype of a scientist was the older White male, thinning hair, glasses and a lab coat. More women are entering the fields of science, technology, engineering, and mathematics (STEM); but they are still predominately male fields with many individuals identifying as White male (Funk & Parker, 2018).). Attending conferences made it difficult to not feel out of place. There's nothing like a heavy pour of stereotype threat with a dash of bitter imposter syndrome chased with the reminder of being a novice to make one question the extent of their capability.

I did what I was raised to do and faked it 'till I made it. I wore make-up, hoping that people would at least view me for my actual age, and always wore professional clothing. I learned to cover my tattoo with eye shadow and reduced the sizes of my piercings. I practiced all my presentations in the mirror and forced myself to see the strength that I knew others saw, even if I didn't always feel it. I took ownership of my novice status and wore it as a badge of exploration. Interacting with experts was a time to "nerd out" and enjoy the learning process. I can't take credit for arriving at this realization alone. As part of the MARC program, I had daily and weekly contact with my MARC Mentor and MARC Director, respectively. Both women presented me with high, yet realistic standards for my work both in and outside the lab. I never felt judged for my lack of knowledge or the amount of effort I put forth to achieve what others seemed to achieve with ease. They embraced my curiosity and questions; they never made me feel that I was smart with a qualifier or that I was provided the opportunity as a racial favor. During my moments of imposter syndrome, I'd look in the mirror and remind myself that these two successful women wouldn't invest their time and reputations into someone who was undeserving of both. More importantly, during my times of doubt, they would push me to excel and acknowledge versus downplay my abilities.

During my first year as a MARC Scholar I earned additional scholarships, paid internships, and travel grants to conferences. I had an epiphany; I was no longer paying for access to education; instead, I was being recruited and paid to acquire and share knowledge. Programs, organizations, and people were investing their time and money to further the advancement of my skills. By the end of my first year in MARC I began identifying as an academic and research scholar. Over time conferences became a place of excitement and enjoyment. Cognitively, I transitioned from a chronic fear of confirming stereotypes and feeling like an imposter to experiencing a sense of confidence and entitlement to entering and thriving in places of excellence.

My cognitive reframing wasn't permanent and over time bouts of stereotype threat and imposter syndrome would find their way back to my thoughts. Even now, fifteen years later as I travel new career paths, I remind myself that being a novice is acceptable. I lost track of this realization in graduate school and spent years working to obtain it back. In graduate school I was implicitly taught that you must always exhibit scholarly qualities; you are an expert at what you do, as if being a novice was evidence of failing versus an opportunity for growth. When I take on new opportunities, I keep the fact that I'm a novice in my forethoughts. During the completion of my PhD, my transition to a tenure-track position, and a career shift out of academia, each transition carried the burden of self-doubt and fear of confirming the doubts of others. During each transition I'd look in the mirror and remind myself that I struggle, strive, then thrive. As a novice I struggle to acquire needed knowledge and skills, strive to apply my unique skill set to be fluent in both, then thrive as I gain more experience.

I'M NOT EVIDENCE OF PROGRESS

I typically hear some functional equivalence of "look at how far we've come" (referring to prejudice and discrimination in the United States), followed by some anecdotal evidence provided from my life. I despise when people reference my life as evidence of reduced racism, sexism, classism, etc., within the United States. If someone like me could be successful and educated, then how could we not view society as making great strides toward equality? How could we not view racial prejudice and discrimination as an issue of the past? I get it; people see degrees, certifications, and wedding and vacation photos with brief updates about my life and view this as evidence of progress. In the span of three generations my family tree went from an eighth-grade education to a PhD. By the age of thirty-three I had three college degrees, was living debt free, owned my house, and took yearly vacations. I am a Black female with natural hair living in the Midwest with a White husband and biracial son. I was hired into a tenure-track faculty position during my first round in the academic job market and had the opportunity to work with students and other faculty of color. When I was ready to shift careers, I had the financial stability and emotional support to do so. True, by most standards I'm thriving and many hurdles along the way could be attributed to the typical growing pains of adolescence, early adulthood, career, and life explorations. False, I am not evidence of societal progress; I'm evidence of progress that needs to be made. I'm evidence of the struggles that continue to be whitewashed to preserve the façade that we are quickly progressing toward equality.

I'm Not Evidence of Progress:
Taste of Safety with a Splash of Privilege

"Privilege: a right, immunity, or benefit enjoyed by a particular person or a restricted group of people beyond the advantages of most" (dictonary.com, n.d.). Within the United States greater light has been shined on the privilege experienced by individuals who identify or are identified as White. While the level of privilege will vary depending on the intersectionality of one's White status (e.g., intersectionality with gender, socioeconomic status, education, etc.; Inwood & Martin, 2008), the range of privilege is vast compared to their ethnic minority counterparts (McIntosh, 1988). I realize I carry a certain level of privilege for being an attractive female, having access to high-quality education, and having lighter skin (outside of California's year-round sun). Yet, more than once I've found myself bitter at the ease of the life of my friends and husband. My husband and close friends report feeling safe walking down the street without fear of racial slurs being thrown by drivers. They feel comfortable leaving their houses without their IDs and don't think twice about taking large purses or diaper bags into stores. They don't have prepared statements for campus police or get anxiety when they [police] walk by. They don't worry about strangers trying to touch their hair or respect their personal space. My friends and husband experience a level of daily privilege I can only dream about or experience on rare and brief occasions. Yet, I'm considered "evidence" of progress and equality. I'm considered evidence of progress even though I must remind my husband that his White privilege won't extend to our sons, and we must raise them accordingly. I'm considered evidence of progress but I'll have to supplement my children's education to ensure their history represents people that look like both their parents. I'm considered evidence of progress even though I expect my husband to play his card of White privilege if I'm ever in doubt about the quality of services I receive medically or our children receive educationally. I'm considered evidence of progress even though I sit on my porch anxious that some prejudiced individual will drive by my nice house and feel the need to put the "nigger in their place." I can't be evidence of progress when I feel unsafe in my own home, country, and predominately White spaces. I can't be evidence of progress while my White counterparts move with substantially less concern, fear, and preparation for potential discriminatory situations.

After college I was accepted into a PhD program at a small predominately White institution in Ohio. I attended events for graduate students of color and for the first time in my life was in a room of thirty-plus academics who looked like me. Soon after my arrival a fellow diverse PhD student advised me to never leave the house without my campus ID. My ID wasn't just to obtain student discounts. My ID legitimized my presence to reduce the chances of me being viewed as a threat. There's safety in having evidence that you belong in a predominantly White space, something to ease the minds of those who may implicitly or explicitly question your intentions or abilities. I needed to do whatever I could to let people know that I was not there to be a problem, a sentiment I later learned was shared by many students of color. From that day forward I always had three cards on my person: driver's license, credit card, and graduate ID. I put college decals on my license plate and purchased campus jackets. During traffic stops I'd find a way to slip in my graduate student status when handing over my information.

Socially, sharing my academic status changed how strangers interacted and conversed with me, as if my words suddenly carried more truth and value. After graduate school I was hired as an acting assistant professor in Indiana (assistant professor after the completion of my PhD). After becoming pregnant with my first son, I regularly swam at the local YMCA followed by a brief stop at the local coffee shop and language center. On one such day I entered the shop and was approached by an older Black woman who, without introduction, began questioning me on whether I had signed up for the local WIC program (Woman, Infant, and Child) or government insurance (she was not a WIC representative). I quickly assured her that I did not financially qualify, nor did I require such services. Her efforts could not be deterred as she continued explaining changes in income requirements needed to qualify for services. I took a deep breath and formally introduced myself as Dr. Costello-Harris, assistant professor at the local university (which I later found out she was attending). I assured her that while I was not bringing in riches, the university did pay well enough for me to know that I did not qualify for financially based services. The woman looked embarrassed and finally let me go on my way.

On the one hand, I appreciate someone showing concern for another who may be in need. On the other hand, I don't appreciate being stereotyped and damn near cornered for one to attempt and validate the effort of their concerns. There is nothing wrong with requiring and obtaining resources such as WIC. There is something wrong with having to give an employment breakdown to convince a stranger that you speak the truth regarding your current circumstances. A few years after the birth of my son I was collecting donations for a service trip to Cartagena, Colombia. I went to the local consignment store where my husband, child, and I frequently shopped and conversed with the owner. On one such occasion I requested clothing donations from the store owner, informing her that I was attending the trip with a fellow professor and could provide the service details. She looked sheepish, agreed to donate items, and then began apologizing for her misconceptions about me. Apparently, during my two years shopping at her store she had assumed I was unemployed, not a stay-at home-mother but unemployed, and she felt ashamed for her assumptions. I shouldn't have been surprised; it was one of the few places in town where I had introduced myself without my professional title or not provided personal details beyond the specifics of my family. It was odd that in that store, for those few minutes of shopping, I just viewed myself as a mother. In that specific space I was not hyperaware of "living while Black," an awareness I carried throughout my typical day; even more so after spending time in predominately brown spaces.

The first time I went to Cartagena, Colombia, I was shocked by the weight I felt being lifted when entering this predominately brown space. For the first time in my life, I was able to walk about without standing out. I didn't carry the paranoia of store owners or employees watching my hands for fear of me stealing. I entered stores and didn't feel the need to transfer any large bags or purses to my husband to carry upon walking through the doors. I was introduced as Dr. Costello-Harris and never once had someone ask if they could just call me Vanessa (except by the White students attending the trip). For that brief time, I had a taste of the privilege my White husband experienced daily. I took walks without fear of racial slurs being thrown. I entered restaurants and stores with feelings of acceptance. The ease in which I could breathe made me realize how restricted and unsafe I felt and feel in the United States. I was angry with the realization that this was how life was supposed to be and how my husband and friends have felt for most of their lives. At the age of thirty-one I felt safe for the first time since becoming aware of my racial difference. In Colombia I felt safe being Black; more importantly I didn't feel unsafe for being Black. The skeptic may believe that I was feeling the typical relaxation of vacation, with the local demographics having no true influence. Yet, this feeling of belonging and safety has yet to be replicated during vacations in predominately White spaces. I weep for a time when I can walk down the streets of my own neighborhood and experience the feeling of safety and acceptance that I felt in a country that was not my own.

I'm Not Evidence of Progress: The Job Search and Academia

As a child I grew up with little thought toward how the "other side" lives, how White women and men may have an easier experience moving through their day: shopping, going to school, or searching for and obtaining employment. Most of my friends were White and seemed to have many of the same goals, fears, and insecurities as myself. Growing up I attributed my daily frustrations to being female versus being Black. In truth, I can't separate my membership within these two groups. My experiences and decisions have always been influenced by my identity as a Black female; a realization I made in adolescence and only became more apparent during college and after meeting my husband. I could no longer ignore the differences in the Black and White experience nor successfully pacify my frustrations.

My husband is a White male with brown hair, blue eyes, and freckles. We both came from low-income backgrounds putting ourselves through school with grants, student loans, and part-time work. I grew up in a large city in Southern California while he grew up in rural Pennsylvania. He grew up in an area with such little diversity that a recent attendance to our niece's graduation resulted in me being one of the two brown faces in the audience. The start and continuation of our relationship has forced both of us to be explicitly aware of the differences and extra hurdles I faced (and continue to face) as a Black female compared to his as a White male. A major difference being the number of academic role models we could encounter who looked like us. I can count on one hand the number of Black PhDs I'd met prior to graduate school and the number hardly grew during my seven years there. While my husband need only to walk into a random classroom and had a high probability of engaging with someone like him. Our experiences can't be a surprise when there's such a disparity in the demographics of PhD recipients. According to the National Center for Science and Engineering Statistics (NCSES, 2021) between 2010 and 2020 a total of 375,830 US citizens and permanent residents received PhDs. Of those PhD recipients, 36% and 35% identified as White males and females, respectively; compared to the 4% and 2% who identified as Black/African American females and males, respectively. These statistics support the uniqueness of our relationship and a rare opportunity to shed light with at least one example of this dichotomous experience.

My husband and I both hold PhDs, in separate fields, and started our careers in tenure-track positions. We went through the job search process four years apart and were both hired at predominantly White institutions (PWI) in the Midwest. He applied after completing his PhD, while I applied when I was "All but Dissertation" (ABD). Our job search experiences included similar concerns; would our curriculum vitas stand out, were our teaching experiences broad enough, our scholarly work strong enough, would we be viewed as qualified, and what should we wear to be viewed as professional? Unfortunately, my job search process included additional concerns. Specifically, should I *whiten* my application packet and if so, how much? The practice of "whitening your résumé" includes removing or downplaying the racial or ethnic cues from one's résumé to decrease potential discrimination during the résumé screening process (Kang, DeCelles, Tilcsik, & Jun, 2016). Kang and colleagues (2016) conducted a three-part study looking at students' rationale for résumé whitening, degrees of whitening, and chances of being offered an interview from real employers. Participants included Black and Asian college students, with 36% of participants reporting engaging in some degree of résumé whitening and two-thirds of the sample knowing a friend or family member who engaged in the practice. The two most common techniques included using less ethnic sounding first names and removing or altering racial cues associated with awards or organization memberships. Students employed fewer résumé whitening techniques when job postings emphasized valuing diversity. Unfortunately, employers were more likely to offer interviews to applicants with greater levels of résumé whitening regardless of the job posting stating they valued diversity. I personally found myself in a *damned if you do, damned if you don't* type of situation. Option 1: whiten my résumé, risk reducing my accomplishments through omission or alteration, and potentially decrease my chances of implicit discrimination. Option 2: don't whiten my résumé, present a stronger application but risk increased chances of implicit discrimination. I chose to roll the dice and not purposefully whiten my résumé, though I assume my background whitened it enough for me.

Vanessa Harris from Southern California and residing in Ohio; insert mental image of a fair-skinned woman here. I've been told that my name and voice both "sound White" (obligatory eye roll here). Thus, unless I disclosed my ethnic minority status, the taste of White privilege my name provided would continue . . . until the onsite interview: "surprise!!" My name alone could make my applications implicitly more palatable for the predominately White search committees. At first glance, my cover letter and CV exhibited few cues regarding my ethnic minority status. Most of my service and scholarly work had been umbrellaed under terms like diversity and inclusion, which also aligned with my academic work on disabilities. I considered expanding on my experiences, providing more details regarding my role and contribution as a Black female, educator, and researcher. On the other hand, I could keep it simple and not draw unnecessary attention to factors that could have me viewed as a less than ideal fit for the campus culture. I consistently asked myself, how much of my story would be watered down if I removed the experiences or details that were driven by my identity as a Black female? Context. I'd be erasing part of my context. I chose to explicitly state my ethnic identity within the first paragraph of my cover letter. For me, this disclosure was the beginning of me taking ownership of my identity as a Black academic.

Decisions to whiten for greater job prospects don't stop after obtaining an interview. Whitening considerations continued through my daily choices of the onsite interview; from the words I used to the details I shared. When preparing for my onsite interview I had anxiety over hairstyles. Should I wear my hair natural, straightened, braided, or some other hairstyle that could be viewed as less Afrocentric and more professional for this predominately White setting? I searched discussion boards and blogs of professional Black women and found that I was not alone in my worries nor paranoid in my beliefs. I'd be more likely to obtain a job interview, be viewed as more professional and competent if I straightened my hair and used standard American English (Koval & Rosette, 2021; McCluney et al., 2021). Would I get extra points if I disclosed my interracial marital status, with a casual picture from my recent travels? Would this connection help me come across as more approachable, similar, or a better fit for the students at the PWI while also being a beacon of safety for ethnic minority students?

My husband never had to consider this whitening process, a fact that changed due to our relationship. When preparing for the onsite interview, my husband received his typical haircut, went shopping for a suit, and sent pictures to his advisor to get feedback on the style and color. He ran through his presentations, potential interview questions, and practiced ways to be personable throughout the onsite visit. Before his campus visit, we had a discussion of first impressions and implicit biases. I reminded him that when he walks onto that campus all the search committee would see is a blue eyed, White male in a nice suit. For better or worse he fit the prototypical image of a Midwest college professor. He looked like someone they could have a beer with or meet at the golf course. His looks and perceived background automatically placed him in the "one of us" category, and care needed to be taken that he stayed there long enough to obtain a job offer. I reminded him of the potential blowback he might experience if he disclosed our relationship during the interview process. Did I expect explicit biases? No, but I am not someone who embraces the idea that "ignorance is bliss" because stepping on a rusty nail hidden in plush carpet can be more harmful than a nail you see coming.

I'm Not Evidence of Progress:
Teaching While Black Before and After Motherhood

I loved teaching in the academic setting, being able to cover a broad range of topics while weaving together a comprehensive story with psychology as the foundation. I embrace the importance of teaching through storytelling and personal examples. However, I had to remind myself that this openness can create a state of vulnerability on the part of the storyteller. Before each lecture I had to take emotional stock of what I could discuss beyond empirical research findings. Which personal examples would I provide, which historical stories and videos would I share? The topics themselves weren't emotionally draining; the exhaustion came from holding back frustrations of society's failings. Society's failings of disproportionally sharing the burden of prejudice and discrimination. Many of my students expressed shock and disbelief that discrimination was still running rampant. I was teaching on topics that I had to learn via life experiences to survive, succeed, and thrive; while others had the privilege to learn just enough to pass a test or write a paper. Part of me believed that sharing my experiences could help right this wrong. Letting students see that even I, an educated Black female, with melanin skin the shade of a well-baked cookie, and only a handful of years older than them, still fight discrimination and navigate a world of prejudice. I wanted them to see that my general experiences and worries were no different than the ethnic minorities depicted in their favorite tv shows and movies. I wanted students to see that I was not evidence of progress. I believed that if even a handful of students could digest the information and move through the world with a greater purpose of equality then my frustrations would be worth it. These beliefs began to shift during the 2016 presidential election.

During the 2016 Trump election, a childhood friend expressed irritation and confusion over the racial divide the election was "causing." He wished we could go back to our time of adolescence when things were simple and race didn't matter. My truth spilled out like a torn bag of rice, messy and unorganized. He was shocked to hear of the struggles my family endured as ethnic minorities and wished we had told him of our struggles as children to remove his own ignorance. I know the statement came from a place of concern and well meaning, but it also came from a place of entitlement. Not once during our conversation did he question why his parents or the school system did not emphasize the hurdles ethnic minorities still face. Yet, he was quick to question why my childhood-self did not make the effort to teach him. He further believed that, as an educator, I should be more than willing to discuss my experiences as a Black individual, both in and outside the classroom. He spoke as if thousands of resources weren't sitting at his fingertips and only by learning of the trials of his peers could he see beyond his own experiences.

Don't believe the struggle is true until someone bares their soul to you. Let me experience pain and sorrow then I'll teach you about it tomorrow.

My friend was right, I am an educator, but as an educator I'm paid to share information within my specialty of study. There were times I reminded myself that my job was to teach psychology and just doing my job did not minimize my commitment. I was not required to, nor paid extra to, share evidence of my Black experience. Yet, there is this underlying expectation in society that individuals who are part of minority groups should share their experiences for free to enhance the knowledge of the majority. Unfortunately, the weight of this burden continues to be picked up by each generation. I observed many of my ethnic minority students share their experiences with the class. Even students who were shy and rarely spoke during the semester tended to share their two cents during discussions of inequality. I appreciated their contributions but not the potential costs. I began pulling these students aside and informing them that, while I appreciated their contributions to the class by speaking up, they were not required to do so. A few of these students reported a sense of responsibility to share their stories as if they were selling the rest of the class short if they did not speak up. I saw a reflection of myself. I told them what I wish someone would have told me, "You do not have to share your scars to benefit the education of others; you owe no one," a lesson I wished to pass to my own children.

Before the birth of my first son, I had no problem standing in front of a class as Dr. Costello-Harris the academic. I would teach on topics of prejudice and discrimination, sharing my stories while keeping my views and emotions a safe distance away. I presented my stories as a neutral onlooker not wanting my emotions and beliefs creating an even more uncomfortable environment for a difficult topic. Then I became a Black mother and experienced the fear and anxiety that accompanies having a Black child. My prenatal anxiety went beyond concerns for the general health and safety of my child but were hyper-focused on his safety as a Black male. I remember the excitement I felt when completing the ultrasound to reveal the sex of our child. I also remember the anxiety and sadness I felt when I realized the life expectancy of my child had just dropped and the challenges he'd face would vary depending on his resemblance to me versus his White father.

With motherhood came the realization that I was no longer just teaching students. I was educating adults whose children would live and learn alongside my own. My child, whom I'm preparing to handle a world that will consistently ask him, "what are you?" I'm preparing him for a world where people believe they can teach children to be "color-blind" and that doing so is a step toward equality. I could no longer teach only as Dr. Costello-Harris the neutral academic. Neutrality no longer felt like a good teaching technique;

instead it felt like another way to whitewash the classroom experience and cater to the feelings of the majority. I was no longer the professor educating the future but the professor and Black mother educating society members who could either harm, protect, embrace, or reject her child. I was educating individuals who would enhance or reduce his safety. I was educating individuals who could make him feel that he was an equal. Being a bystander was no longer an option. Trying to present neutrality was no longer an option. Black female faculty at PWI report feeling that students put them in two roles, the "Mammy Caregiver" or the "Angry Black Woman" (Harlow, 2003). Being concerned that I would be interpreted as the angry Black woman was no longer an option—because I was angry. Angry at the fact that I had to be so scared for my child and his future. Angry that I already had to have this heightened awareness of the dangers that he'll likely be exposed to. Angry that I have to teach my husband to identify and navigate these situations in case I'm not around to help him do so. Angry for the day that my son comes home after hearing the word nigger and starts to notice that people treat him differently. No, I'm not evidence of progress.

CALL ME BY THE NAME I GIVE YOU

The names and titles we choose to use matter and so do the names and titles people choose to address us by. Students are more likely to address male professors by their professional titles than their female counterparts (Takiff, Sanchez, & Stewart, 2001). Takiff and colleagues (2001) further reported that professors addressed by their professional titles (regardless of gender) were viewed as holding greater status at the university. Unfortunately, female professors addressed by their professional title were also viewed as less accessible, a situation experienced less often by their male counterparts. For females, being addressed by your title can be a double-edged sword. Insisting that others use your title can be just as risky, with 20% of students reporting negative reactions to professors who informed students of their preferred form of address (Hildenbrand, Perrault, & Devine, 2020).

> Welcome to the class. I'm Dr. Costello-Harris. You can blame my husband for the long name, nonetheless, I do go by my full name. I will also answer to professor, or "excuse me" with great eye contact. While some professors go by their first name, I'm not one of them. I am married, but out of all the titles I could use my relationship status is the least interesting and in no context should I be called Mrs. anything.

The previous narrative was the general statement I would give at the beginning of each semester and every semester I'd have a handful of students insisting on calling me by my first name and questioning their right to do so. Over the years I've had dozens of people ask me why I make such a big deal about the name to which I'm referred. Over the years my answers have changed but one aspect has stayed the same: "because it's the name I gave you." I expect people to respect me enough to call me by the name I give them and not by the name they feel entitled to use. Please keep my wrong name out of your mouth.

Call Me by the Name I Give You: The Academic Setting

In my family names matter, they set the tone for your interactions and remind you how to behave within that context. The name and title I present sets an expectation for my social interactions and in some cases reduces the amount of "junk" people expect me to tolerate. I started teaching full time at the age of twenty-seven and looked as young as most of my eighteen- to twenty-year-old students and was the same age as many of my students in my upper-level courses. I was finishing my PhD and decided to go by Professor Costello-Harris. While I wanted to be viewed as welcoming and approachable, I didn't want to be misclassified as a friend or peer; an issue I felt I experienced while teaching in graduate school. Using my title helped to hold me separate and provide clearer boundaries for my students.

My decision to use the "Professor" title was substantially easier than using the title of "Doctor," mainly due to the emotional trauma I associated with my PhD. Unlike my MARC Scholar experience, which left me feeling empowered and capable of tackling new challenges, graduate school left me with anxiety and self-doubt. Hearing "Dr. Costello-Harris" left a bad taste in my mouth and was a constant reminder of the unhealthy environment I wish I had left sooner. I resented the title I had achieved and many of the experiences that went along with it. My new title was just a reminder of those experiences and a point of time when I felt I lost sight of who I was as a person and scholar. Luckily, my new place of employment was a healthier and a more supportive environment than my graduate school location.

I was especially fortunate to have a colleague and fellow female PhD of color who was always willing to be my sounding board and helped me regain ownership of what I emotionally lost during graduate school. I expressed my internal conflict with using my upgraded title. I knew completing my degree was a major accomplishment and with that came the honor of this new title, but for me the title was never my goal. My goal was to achieve the skills required to obtain the PhD title versus aspiring simply to have a PhD. At the end of the day being referred to as "Doctor" neither added to nor took away from the knowledge and skills I acquired. Then I had a conversation with my colleague who identified the true impact that using my title could have, beyond being treated differently in casual and profession spaces (i.e., as if I have some level of competence), my explicit representation as a female PhD of color was something our students of color needed to encounter. White students have endless examples of successful people who look like them in the classroom, they are surrounded by evidence that people who look like them can be academically successful. Students of color don't have the same luxury, especially students at PWI living in predominately White areas. For many students I would be one of a handful of professors who looked like them and only one of an even smaller number who carried a PhD. Using my title isn't about showing off or feeling entitled but about showing up as a role model to students like me; I use my title for them. To this day my degree is buried under a pile of papers in my home office and still makes me frustrated to look at it but I can now carry and use the "Doctor" title with pride. Less for pride in my accomplishments and more for pride in being able to stand out for future students and professionals like me.

In 2019 I made the hard decision to leave my tenure-track position and for the first time have a career outside of academia. I loved teaching and working with my current students. My colleagues were supportive, I had the freedom to teach classes the way I wanted and yet, I decided to resign. I resigned for two main reasons. First, I needed greater work-life balance, which was no one's fault but my own: to teach the way I wanted, to research the way I wanted, I had to put in a lot of time outside the office. I could only count one vacation in ten years when I didn't take work with me and that was for my honeymoon. I caught myself trying to justify my time to relax and getting frustrated when my two year old interrupted my grading to play. I never viewed myself as a workaholic. During undergraduate school it was easy for me to disconnect from school; I still felt the pressure of work to be done, but also knew and embraced the importance of decompressing. Then graduate school became a race with very few breaks and healthy outlets. Attempts to relax were praised one minute then judged the next for not taking my work seriously enough. I slowly focused more on school and made less time for things outside of academia; something that I continued during my tenure-track position. I had such a strong association between academia and constantly working, I felt the only way to change my behavior was to change my environment.

Call Me by the Name I Give You: The Non-Academic Setting

My second reason for resigning was that I always wanted to get back into applied and community-based work. I started working with individuals and families with special needs when I was eighteen years old. I was employed as a camp counselor, adult day caregiver, and an after-school caregiver. I transitioned out of my community-based job when I was accepted into the MARC program. I shifted from working with clients and providing direct services to conducting research to help inform program staff, community members, and other academics of the resource needs and experiences of the populations they worked with. My scholarly work was important and brought me a level of satisfaction but, like most research, it wasn't having an immediate impact on current practices. It's estimated that it takes up to seventeen years to move information from research to practice (Morris, Wooding, & Grant, 2011), assuming the community members have access to the information and the skills necessary to implement. I had the opportunity to leave academia, transition careers, and use my skills in an applied setting, working directly with clients and their families. Still, I struggled with the idea of removing a Black voice and face from in front of the classroom. I hated the idea of one less PhD of color for our students. Once again, my colleague helped me see the impact I could have this time outside of the classroom. It's just as important to have Black representation outside of the academic setting.

My career transition was difficult for many reasons, one of which was going from a position and area of my expertise to being a novice. I was uncomfortable using my professional name in my new career outside of academia where everyone went by their first names. Being referred to as "Doctor" also set a level of expectation regarding my skill set in this new arena. While I could accept my novice status, I felt that others could not and held the expectation that I would acquire new skills and information quicker than most, regardless of how I was being taught. Simple mistakes such as misspelled words or laps in knowledge would be jokingly followed by, "you're the one with a PhD" or "you're the professor," an emphasis I believe was only made worse by my insisting on not being referred to by my first name.

Dealing with the push-back of others has pushed me to reflect on my current reasons for going by my professional name even when it makes me and those around me uncomfortable. I'm sure some individuals view the use of my title as evidence that I'm stuck up, cocky, entitled, or view myself as better or smarter than those with fewer degrees. I briefly considered giving in to the pressure, working on fitting in, and going by my first name to help me be viewed as more approachable. I'm sure if I was a man, especially a White man, I wouldn't have to give my title a second thought, I know my husband never has. At the end of the day, I know my reasons but my reasons don't matter. Explaining my reasons have rarely reduced the discomfort or push-back I receive when I emphasize my name preference. I've realized the discomfort others feel with my title isn't my problem and it's not my job to take ownership in making them comfortable with the name I use. Others' discomfort isn't a reflection of my beliefs. It's a reflection of theirs and shines a light on a discomfort they need to examine further, without my assistance, all while referring to me by the name I give them. Let me reintroduce myself, I'm Dr. Costello-Harris.

CONCLUSION

Healthy Relationships

Over the years I've learned to thrive in predominately White spaces. I've thrived not as a flower planted in rich soil with plenty of sun and water, but as a flower searching for adequate access to the sun. With every rain fall of potential and support, I pushed against the concrete that attempted to block me from growing toward my fullest potential. A bitter-sweet realization. Bitter because I wonder how much more I would have accomplished or even how less burdened I would've felt during my journey. Sweet because I see that regardless of the unbalanced world around me, I can add my name to the list of Black/African American women who are making a change for the future. Nonetheless, there are parts of my journey that I wish had gone differently and other parts that I wish I had appreciated more along the way.

I wish I had known more people who looked like me during adolescence and throughout my career. As I youth I didn't think the lack of representation mattered, I had enough successful people in my family to see that I was more than capable of accomplishing what I wanted but my scope was limited, especially as I entered graduate school and the academic world. I needed someone who looked like me, who had a similar background, and who had followed the path I was currently traveling. Most importantly I needed someone who met those qualifications, was emotionally healthy, and had the work-life balance I was hoping to achieve. I needed evidence that my goals were possible and some type of breadcrumbs to help me get there. I needed an ear to validate my feelings and experiences and help me not feel "crazy" along the way.

My first piece of advice to people like me who grew up in and continue to find themselves in predominately White spaces: search out people like you while embracing healthy relationships and mentors, regardless of their demographics. The search will be difficult, and you may only find one compatible relationship out of every ten interactions, but the search is necessary and worth it. I made one such connection with a fellow chapter contributor whom I met outside our local gym. My husband jokingly suggested I go introduce myself, as if us both being young Black females with children was enough to start a conversation. I awkwardly introduced myself, using my son as my wingman, and invited them to join us at the library down the street for the "read to paws" activity. Both of our children were clearly too young to be reading, I was sure I scared her off but ten minutes later she and her daughter rolled up to join us. We saw each other almost every weekend for a year and a half (until Covid-19 emerged) and our children became best friends. Oddly enough, we both held degrees in psychology and had similar interests. Most importantly I saw what I can only assume others saw when looking at me: a very intelligent, motivated, successful young woman doing her best in this broken world and was thriving during the process. Unfortunately, like most of my friendships I began to neglect our relationship once I became too busy. My life became a schedule of to-do lists and months flew by like dandelions on a windy day.

I've worked hard to teach myself how to be selfish with my time, and my physical and emotional resources. I grew up seeing women like me endlessly give to support the survival or success of others with little left for themselves and still be willing to give more. I refused to be like *The Giving Tree*, unconditionally giving pieces of myself to better the life of another, while I'm left with nothing but a cut-down version of myself; a stump for others to rest on. I don't regret being selfish, it was a necessary type of self-preservation. It's allowed me the strength to remove myself from unhealthy relationships with the unfortunate side-effect of losing track of my heathy ones. My second piece of advice: make time for healthy relationships while cutting ties with unhealthy ones. Keep and nourish friendships that support you and your goals regardless of the paths you take. I've been negligent of mine and must make a conscious effort to stay connected. Most roads to success are lonely ones but that doesn't mean you are truly alone. I've been lucky enough to have friends who refuse to get rid of me even during times when I was lost in my studies or career. Surround yourself with people who support you, your journey, and the sacrifices you make for those choices. Surround yourself with people who celebrate your successes versus mocking them. This goes for your friends and partners. Have a partner(s) who isn't intimidated by your aspirations or achievements, who believes that your career is just as important as theirs, and treats your goals accordingly. My husband has been a constant source of healthy support during my journey through graduate school, academia, motherhood, and career shifts. More days than not I notice the extra work he does to help us achieve both our career and personal goals. My husband is amazing, and I appreciate all that he's done, does, and will do; but the truth is, getting to this point took work and honesty. I had to be honest from the beginning about my family and career goals. I had to be honest with myself and then honest with him about my expectations and fears. Most importantly, I pushed him to be honest with himself about what he wanted and would be willing to compromise or sacrifice. We both had to learn the difference between doing everything we *could do* versus making time for things we *wanted* to do; and extending this idea from the home into our careers.

I Can Do It, But I Don't Want To

"You are a strong Black woman and come from a line of strong Black women, you are capable of more than you think and will be successful in the end." This is what I would tell myself during my times of struggle. I embraced the idea of being a strong Black woman like you'd embrace a safety blanket. Struggle, strive, and thrive; that was my rhythm that I danced toward success. During my times of failing, my family and friends would remind me of all that I had already accomplished, overcome, and the hard work I had put in. What was one more hurdle? So, I'm here to tell you this: you *can* handle what the world throws at you, you *can* face any challenge, and *can* achieve things beyond your dreams or imagination. But you must identify the difference between doing what you *can* versus what you *want*. Being able to achieve a goal is not and should not be enough, you also want to be in a healthy state when it's over. I always viewed myself as being strong enough to push through, strong enough to move beyond anxiety, depression, and general self-doubt. There were times when I wore myself down physically and emotionally to achieve goals that later I realized had very little value to me; but switching paths would be equivalent to failing.

My friends and family saw me as the Strong Black Woman and so did I; until one day I could hardly look in the mirror because all I saw was exhaustion and failings. For years my body told me to slow down, but I pushed through and prevailed. "Mind over matter" or "what doesn't kill you makes you stronger," these are the mantras people hurled at me. I tried to embrace these mantras until I broke out in a full body rash from the stress I was under. I was covered in bumps and peeling skin from head to toe, my body itched, and it hurt to move. The only thing that made me cry more than taking a bath was looking in the mirror, mainly because I had done this to myself. It took two months to regain some level of physical normalcy, but ten years later I still carry the physical and emotional scars. Scars that remind me that, yes, I had pushed, overcome, and achieved; but at what cost? It's taken time and I'm still working on it but I've had to redefine what it means to be a strong Black woman. Survival and struggle are no longer part of my definition. I will no longer be pressured, shamed, or guilted into putting more on my plate just because I can.

I've rejected the view of strength being evident by stretching myself to my limits. I'm not strong because I take on extra burdens and the burdens of those around me. I'm not a success for swallowing my grief and pain stoically, putting more on my plate because of not wanting to disappoint others, or wanting to maintain the perception of ability and strength. No, my definition includes identifying the difference between what I *can* do and what I *want* to do. I *can* take on an extra project or join an additional committee and a part of me wouldn't mind contributing, yes, I can do it. Am I at risk of stretching myself to the point of diminished returns? If the answer is anything other than no, then I don't need to add another task, most importantly I don't want one. Graduate school and my early time in academia was spent doing a lot of what I could do versus wanted to do. I could apply for additional grants, take on more people to mentor, or volunteer more of my time. I wanted to be viewed as valuable, carrying my weight, being just as productive as those around me regardless of my years of experience. I wanted everyone to realize, myself included, that I could hold my own and needed no qualifiers. I realize now that I am and always have been valuable. I've always carried my own weight but I'll decide how heavy the load is and what is an acceptable burden to carry. I can handle anything but I have no desire to. I will not measure my success by the struggles I've overcome or barriers I break down. I will not define myself by another's metric system. I value who I am now but I also want to value who I'll be in the future. I now make decisions for my future self and well-being. I protect myself by helping my friends and family accept my new definition of the Strong Black Woman and showing them the difference between supporting me to succeed versus pressuring me to overcome. I protect myself by making sure I have the physical, mental, and emotional strength to complete the tasks I want to do versus completing all the tasks I can do. I am a strong Black woman, strong enough to say "No" and strong enough to know and make others acknowledge my worth. I will not measure my worth by the buckets of tears I carry along my journey but by the number of buckets I learn to put down or not pick up along the way. I am a strong Black woman because I have the strength to say when enough is enough; and you do too. Put down your burdens and expectations from others, or even the burdens you place on yourself. I'm here to tell you, you are a strong Black woman and you are enough.

REFERENCES

Clance, P. R., & Imes, S. A. (1978). The imposter phenomenon in high achieving women: Dynamics and therapeutic intervention. *Psychotherapy: Theory, research & practice, 15*(3), 241.

Crenshaw, K. (1989). Demarginalizing the intersection of race and sex: A Black feminist critique of antidiscrimination doctrine, feminist theory and antiracist politics. *u. Chi. Legal f.*, 139.

Du Bois, W. E. B. (1903). *The Souls of Black Folks.* A. C. McClurg & Sons.

Funk, C., & Parker, K. (2018). Women and men in STEM often at odds over workplace equity. Washington, DC: Pew Research Center. Retrieved from www.pewresearch.org/social-trends/2018/01/09/diversity-in-the-stem-workforce-varies-widely-across-jobs/.

Harlow, R. (2003). "Race doesn't matter, but . . . ": The effect of race on professors' experiences and emotion management in the undergraduate college classroom. *Social psychology quarterly*, 348–363.

Hildenbrand, G. M., Perrault, E. K., & Devine, T. M. (2020). You may call me professor: Professor form of address in email communication and college student reactions to not knowing what to call their professors. *Journal of Communication Pedagogy, 3*, 82–99.

Holoien, D. S., & Shelton, J. N. (2012). You deplete me: The cognitive costs of color-blindness on ethnic minorities. *Journal of Experimental Social Psychology, 48*(2), 562–565.

Inwood, J. F., & Martin, D. G. (2008). Whitewash: White privilege and racialized landscapes at the University of Georgia. *Social & Cultural Geography, 9*(4), 373–395.

Kang, S. K., DeCelles, K. A., Tilcsik, A., & Jun, S. (2016). Whitened résumés: Race and self-presentation in the labor market. *Administrative Science Quarterly, 61*(3), 469–502.

Koval, C. Z., & Rosette, A. S. (2021). The natural hair bias in job recruitment. *Social Psychological and Personality Science, 12*(5), 741–750.

Leu, K. (2017). Beginning college students who change their majors within 3 years of enrollment. Data Point. NCES 2018–44. *National Center for Education Statistics*.

McCluney, C. L., Durkee, M. I., Smith II, R. E., Robotham, K. J., & Lee, S. S. L. (2021). To be, or not to be . . . Black: The effects of racial codeswitching on perceived professionalism in the workplace. *Journal of experimental social psychology, 97*, 104199.

McIntosh, P. (1988). *White privilege and male privilege: A personal account of coming to see correspondences through work in women's studies*, Volume 189. Wellesley, MA: Wellesley College, Center for Research on Women.

Morris, Z. S., Wooding, S., & Grant, J. (2011). The answer is 17 years, what is the question: understanding time lags in translational research. *Journal of the Royal Society of Medicine, 104*(12), 510–520.

National Center for Science and Engineering Statistics. (2021, November 30). *Doctorate Recipients from U.S. Universities: 2020* (NSF-22–300). Alexandria, VA: National Science Foundation. Retrieved from ncses.nsf.gov/pubs/nsf22300/data-tables.

Peteet, B. J., Montgomery, L., & Weekes, J. C. (2015). Predictors of imposter phenomenon among talented ethnic minority undergraduate students. *The Journal of Negro Education, 84*(2), 175–186.

Privilege. (n.d.). In *Dictionary online dictionary*. Retrieved from www.dictionary.com/browse/privilege.

Ross, T., Kena, G., Rathbun, A., Kewal Ramani, A., Zhang, J., Kristapovich, P., & Manning, E. (2012). *Higher education: Gaps in access and persistence study. Statistical analysis report* (NCES 2012–046). National Center for Education Statistics. Retrieved from nces.ed.gov/pubs2012/2012046.pdf.

Solórzano, D., Ceja, M., & Yosso, T. (2000). Critical race theory, racial microaggressions, and campus racial climate: The experiences of African American college students. *Journal of Negro education*, 60–73.

Steele, C. M., & Aronson, J. (1995). Stereotype threat and the intellectual test performance of African Americans. *Journal of personality and social psychology, 69*(5), 797.

Sue, D. W., Capodilupo, C. M., Torino, G. C., Bucceri, J. M., Holder, A., Nadal, K. L., & Esquilin, M. (2007). Racial microaggressions in everyday life: Implications for clinical practice. *American Psychologist, 62*(4), 271.

Takiff, H. A., Sanchez, D. T., & Stewart, T. L. (2001). What's in a name? The status implications of students' terms of address for male and female professors. *Psychology of Women Quarterly, 25*(2), 134–144.

Thomas, A. J., Hacker, J. D., & Hoxha, D. (2011). Gendered racial identity of Black young women. *Sex Roles, 64*(7–8), 530–542.

US Census Bureau. (2021, October 19). *Census Bureau data reveal decline in school enrollment* (Report No. CB21-TPS.120). Retrieved from www.census.gov/newsroom/press-releases/2021/decline-school-enrollment.html.

US Department of Education. Office for Civil Rights. (2016). *2013–2014 Civil Rights data collection: A first look; June 7, 2016 report*. Retrieved from the US Department of Education website: www2.ed.gov/about/offices/list/ocr/docs/2013-14-first-look.pdf.

Chapter 6

This Is America

Rosalyn D. Davis

Almost two years ago, I was brought together with a dynamic young woman to present at the first virtual social justice conference that our university was sponsoring. I don't know that either of us was completely clear on how we had been selected as someone who would be good to speak on anything, but we were only told that we had a set amount of time, a moderator, and free reign to discuss whatever we liked. I am not sure that you should ever tell that to folks in mental health professions, but especially not at the time we were brought together. Since this is being written well after the moments of that summer it may sound like a detached retelling of both that experience and what came of it. You are likely wondering who we were, so let me (Rosalyn) briefly introduce the us in question as Maqubè Reese, MSW, and Dr. Rosalyn Davis. We did not know each other before this collaboration but when the opportunity for this book was presented to me, there was no way that I didn't want to touch on what we created together. The rest of this chapter will incorporate my thoughts and some of framework that Maqubè was kind enough to share with me as we were creating our presentation.

Let's begin at the beginning. We were firmly in the pandemic when we were brought together. The world was begrudgingly going along with a lockdown as we watched the death toll continue to climb and we had neither a vaccine nor reasonable treatments to tackle the disease. We also had leadership that was not being honest about the disease and what would be needed to fight it. That led to unnecessary death and politicization of a health crisis. We couldn't be like New Zealand who told everyone to sit down and chill out. We restricted travel later than we probably should have and we didn't want to sacrifice for anyone that we didn't have to. I am using the global "we" here. This isn't about the legions of us who may have been tired of Zoom meetings when we met but who were chilling at home.

Our initial meeting was also shortly after the televised murder of George Floyd at the hands of police in Minneapolis, as well as the reports of the deaths of Breonna Taylor during a no-knock warrant looking for someone who didn't live at her apartment and of Ahmaud Arbery by Travis McMichael, his father Gregory, and friend William Bryan. Each of these murders was jarring but even more so because while we couldn't go anywhere really, it proved many times over that Black people weren't safe at home or close to home. However, the most interesting thing for me about that moment in time was that people actually seemed to be shocked by the reports on each death. By people, I don't mean the Black, Indigenous, or other People of Color (BIPoC) in the United States. That group of people, along with a large swath of the LGBTQ folks, were all likely thinking nothing about those moments were new except the video, and really not even then.

There has been video of police behaving badly going back to Rodney King, and it resulted in nothing but an acquittal of the officers who beat Mr. King so badly that it most likely shortened his life. But white people were horrified; and not just white people in the United States. George Floyd's murder set off global protests in countries that had their own racial trauma they need to sort out, and others that just wanted to be supportive. It was intriguing to watch and process the greater events as we worked together to decide on a theme for our presentation. One thing came up for both of us: the reaction of the students we were working with who seemed legitimately dumbfounded by the level of violence they had been able to avoid noticing in marginalized communities. They had bought into the narrative that if you just complied with officers that all would be well, even though again, there's been video of literally no provocation leading to the death of unarmed or legally armed Black and Brown people. As we spoke, one of us expressed incredulity about the lack of understanding or belief or whatever it was that was leading to the shock and awe of our students while the other responded that, no, this is America and this is always who America has been.

Thus we found the theme for our presentation. We were going to talk about America honestly and what the audience could do to try to make things better. We came up with a brief agenda and then some points we wanted to cover over the course of the presentation. We also agreed to share in the moment if something else moved us to do so. The rest of this chapter will focus on that presentation and what we may have added if we were going to redo this presentation right now. Buckle up and brace yourselves for the very raw and necessary dialogue that took place on a January morning in 2021.

THIS IS AMERICA: TEACHING AN ACCURATE REFLECTION OF DIVERSITY EQUITY AND INCLUSION

An Introduction

I am going to keep this section brief because you can read our future biographies if you really want to know more. Maqubè Reese (Ma-quee-ba) Reese, MSW, is a social justice strategist, consultant, and a higher education DEIJB thought leader. Maqubè holds a master of social work degree from the Indiana University Purdue University Indianapolis School of Social Work and a BS degree from Indiana University Bloomington. Currently, her work includes anti-racist training through her consulting company, Tribe Consulting. She is heavily involved in community engagement on a local, state, and federal level. Dr. Rosalyn Davis is a clinical associate professor of psychology, director of the Mental Health Counseling Program, affirmative action liaison, and faculty diversity liaison at Indiana University Kokomo where she has worked since 2013. She holds a doctorate in counseling psychology from Ball State University, master's in Counseling from the University of Texas at San Antonio, and BA degree in psychology from Fisk University. Her work includes teaching clinical courses and speaking on areas of diversity, equity, and inclusion in psychology and education at the local, state, regional, and national levels.

What Is DEI and What Is It Not?

This didn't strike us as something that needed to be discussed until we met a few times. People had at the time, and likely more so now, begun to think of diversity, equity, and inclusion work as tied to (1) making people feel bad and (2) taking jobs or opportunities away from people who were not included under the DEI umbrella. There is no DEI educator or trainer who would tell you that is the work we do. We don't have the power to do the second part and if the first part happens it is unintended. DEI work is largely about sharing information and trying to make sure the world we live and work in is equally available to everyone who exists in it. When we address diversity, we do so to include more than just race and ethnicity, even though those are the easiest points to visually see and unfortunately conflate. You can be ethnically diverse and racially present as white, and you can be racially diverse and have no ethnicity that you directly relate to as an individual or community. Equity typically means that we are planning to implement change that will benefit large segments of the population. For a smaller group, it means that they may be losing something and that is more important than what others may be gaining. Finally, there's inclusion, which for most DEI workers really just means how can we make the spaces we live and work in as accessible as possible to people. We need to know about ability status, religion, and socioeconomic status just as much as we need to understand racial similarities or differences. We didn't include justice because that would really mean a whole different presentation that we knew we didn't have time for but that's equity on steroids and making sure previous wrongs are not continued, acknowledging the harm that was done, and rectifying the situation as thoroughly as possible.

This was likely the least controversial thing we discussed. Our basic definitions of the work we do and how to all be on the same page before we went forward with the presentation. At this point, everyone was still calm and there were no questions waiting for us. I believe if we were to revisit this presentation now we'd likely delve into the conversation about justice because it has come up in a number of criminal cases in the last few years to address some of the harm that was done by white perpetrators against individuals of color.

How Do We Acknowledge Our Own Biases?

There is probably nothing that makes people more uncomfortable in DEI trainings than admitting to their own biases or blind spots. However, we all have them, and we need to acknowledge how they may interfere with our work. As a military brat I got very used to relocating every few years and meeting new people. That is great for developing flexibility around culture and getting to know people who don't look like me. As great as that is in terms of meeting new people, it created a blind spot for me that I wasn't aware of until internship. It was then that I met people who have never left their home state in their entire lives. For folks at my next job, though, being three hours away from home was so far away that they struggled to remain in school. These struggles were foreign to me, and I really had to wrap my head around that kind of fear of the unknown. Not sure why that had never occurred to me, but hopping on a plane for a new job or the fact that it may take a day to drive across my home state were normal to me. That is not normal to a large percentage of the population.

The exercise that I offered up to our audience was to do a self-check often. A self-check, in this case, is to write down all of their personality traits that they were proud of and thought made them unique. Then they should spend time thinking about what was fantastic about those traits as well as what may be limiting about those traits. Those limitations would likely be their biases or blind spots. My parents are divorced, but they gave my siblings and me so much attention that it was annoying; therefore, bad or neglectful parents are a bias point for me. This is not an exercise to do once and assume it doesn't need to be done again. Whenever there is a life event or change, we need to revisit that list and see where we might have changed. I have loved to assign this exercise for years, as it tends to work very well in group settings. In addition, it is easier to encourage individuals to reframe their thinking than it is to call them racist if they haven't thought about these things on their own.

How Do We Help Others with Their Biases?

The benefit of being in education is that you can do things that deliberately make people feel uncomfortable while also building in ways to address that discomfort, with the goal of creating growth. For example, if you give a group of people an assessment or exam that they are designed to fail with the intent of opening them to the next wave of assignments or experiences, that's just planning ahead and not tormenting them for no good reason. Good educators know that people tend to learn more when they are uncomfortable. Being asked to do something that seems problematic to their personal viewpoints is a primary point of discomfort. People hate the exercise and often say that it makes them feel racist because they are using limited visual cues to assign racial designations to a pool of twenty faces. We address that by asking how it is different from what we do daily when we see people we do not know out in the world. There's often a pause and then a moment of realization that it is not different. We make snap judgments about other people based on limited information that may not reflect reality. We are especially bad at snap judgments when the people are from totally different cultures or racial groups. As we lead the group through these uncomfortable conversations, the group discusses what it means to misidentify someone, how that may impact our work, and what we can do to address it. They recognize that the easiest thing to do is interact with more people from those unfamiliar groups, but they also acknowledge some trepidation at the thought of those interactions. One solution is to explore these tenuous interactions in settings that are not likely to cause irreparable harm. For example, we suggest trying a new restaurant and asking about the culture. Another possibility is to take in a service in an unfamiliar religious institution to see what you share and what you don't. A third idea might be taking a trip and participating in activities that are new and slightly unfamiliar.

Of course, at the time of our presentation the world was closed so almost none of these suggestions could easily be implemented. While it is possible now, individuals still must take into account their risk tolerance level with the ongoing pandemic. The suggestions likely wouldn't change, but they would be modified to include the following reminder. Members of diverse communities do not owe anyone access to their culture. If they don't want to engage with you, it doesn't matter how genuine your interest is in learning about their culture or community. We have found an amazing point of connection when people meet over dinner. Discussing what we do when we celebrate holidays, travel, have no time or on our hands, or need a figurative hug is one of the most available entry points to us. So, check out that new restaurant, ask your colleague about a traditional holiday dish, or bring something of yourself to those who would be willing to partake and see what happens. However, let us share a few words of warning. There has been a long history of people observing and minimizing BIPOC because they do not culturally line up with the dominant culture. First, as you explore, try not to do so as from a deficit mindset and devalue what you are experiencing because it's not what you are used to in your regular life (Roberts-Miller, 2019). Second, I (Rosalyn) shared with the group that I know Juneteenth is a new holiday for a lot of people, so you may be interested or inclined to look for guidance on how to celebrate the day. As a native Texan, where the holiday originated, we do not have a "traditional" menu or set of activities. It really is a day to acknowledge what took place, feed those I love something delicious, and make sure that I do not go to work.

How to Create Buy-In

This was a brief point of discussion during the workshop. The world runs better when it involves hearing from lots of different people. Hearing from lots of people and pausing, not trying to enforce a particular narrative, and not forcing and particular dialogue to transpire. There comes a point in time where you find and make peace with you. The United States has to recognize the injustices that are frequently visited upon communities of color and show not only disparate treatment but ongoing inequities that widen the gap in quality of life for those communities. This point of discussion is to maintain the conversation, but in a way that inspires systemic change. It must be systemic because goals are short lived, systems are legacy or sustainable. Hire that consultant, have the discussion, and put "professional development funding" in your annual and ongoing budget. Be clear, though, that if you are hiring a consultant, that person should be more than a person of color or someone who is passionate about diversity, equity, and inclusion. What training do they report to have? What kind of work do you need and can that person deliver what you need? A potential consultant may be great at working with educational settings but have little experience with community-based settings. Someone may really know how to tackle DEI in STEM but not knowledgeable about DEI in relation to mental health. Do not hire someone external unless you need to do so, that is, if there is no knowledgeable internal consultant. However, just because an internal consultant is identified to do the necessary DEI work, as an employer you still need to compensate that person for the new and potentially contentious work they are taking on.

How Do I Do This Work Well?

The next topic areas will be collapsed for the sake of clarity because they all relate to the same thing. It is entirely understandable and expected that faculty may be nervous or anxious about teaching topics related to diversity, equity, and inclusion, especially in the current climate. Around the time period of our original presentation, someone had created a website that was targeting faculty teaching DEI in their courses. We won't drive traffic to that site in this work, but it allowed anyone to report faculty who made students uncomfortable or who students felt were biased against conservative values. As you might imagine, like other faculty and professional staff who do this work, we knew our work could be targeted by this website, and honestly, we were afraid of what being added to such a site would do to us personally or professionally. I have to give my campus colleagues massive credit for approaching this situation head-on. Several branch campuses took it upon themselves to add their entire faculty body to the site. Others discussed it on their campus webpages or in syllabi. What no one did, though, was stop teaching. It benefits no one when we are afraid for our safety. It makes one side look like bullies and the other side can rightfully cite infringement on their ability to do their jobs well. We acknowledge that fear may be part of the process, but we need to do some of this afraid to make sure it gets done.

We also know that some students respond better to hearing directly from BIPOC and other minoritized faculty when it comes to issues relating to DEI. It would be wonderful if each student who wanted to do so could learn directly from someone in those populations. The problem is there are not enough people available from those groups to do that work unless they did literally nothing else. That means that some white, cisgender, heterosexual, economically advantaged individuals will also be part of this educational process. Those voices are valuable because there is another group of students that cannot connect with communities of color on these topics. They may be embarrassed about what they don't know, nervous that they may make a mistake, or just not feeling equipped to have conversations with people who do not look like them. You can share your content with them, introduce them to scholars and professionals of color who discuss DEI issues, and you can challenge them to step out of their comfort zone without it feeling like a jarring experience.

Finally, as you or your students are learning more about certain subjects, do not require those from minoritized populations to share their pain with you in order to see their humanity or listen to their stories. At the beginning of this chapter, we discussed that we were brought together in the wake of the George Floyd murder. Even though BIPOC and minoritized Americans had often discussed the ways in which they had been dehumanized and threatened during their interactions with law enforcement, it was often met with some level of pushback from members of the dominant community. Conversations about compliance with orders, previous criminal records, expired tags, lateness of the hour, and fear from the officers involved abounded whenever something violent happened within the impacted communities. The pandemic seemed to strip away the whataboutism because we could no longer deny what had transpired in front of the collective audience. It was like a wound opening up in front of the world and no one questioned if this was wrong. Well let's not say no one but the questions were much less intensive. However, as time has slipped forward and the world has sped back up, people have forgotten what they were so sure of a few short years ago. People have jumped to support the Ukrainian people in their fight against Russia. That's great and should be applauded. They have been less supportive of the Black refugees who were in Ukraine and who were denied entry as their white countrymen fled to receptive nations (Horton, 2022). Americans have done that with other countries as well, but have forgotten that Flint, Michigan, still has lead in the drinking water that we do not seem at all motivated to remove (Goetz, 2022). Communities of color should not have to constantly trumpet their pain for people to care about making them whole. Try to make sure that you don't perpetuate that painful performance play in your training and conversations.

Finally, it helps everyone to connect some of these very amorphous concepts to the real world. We can mention systemic racism to a group of people, and most will have a different understanding of what that is based on what they have heard before. Instead of hoping the definition you provide is clear, take the time to break that down into simpler terms. Your Black college-educated alumnus will likely make the same or slightly less on average than a White high school graduate. It's not just because they will be offered different salaries but because income may be suppressed in communities of color, which then impacts the price of housing, which then impacts the tax base, which then impacts public schools in the area, which then impacts the students who could potentially be admitted to college and make the same as they would from the kids in the neighboring school district who had none of the same challenges. That is clear and concrete, and honestly inexcusable for most of us in a way that saying systemic racism exists and is a problem is not always as clear. Allow the room to be uncomfortable as you make your connections and ask for their impression of the examples you put before them. One of our favorite real-world tie-ins relates to music. College students may not check their email often enough for our tastes, but they know what kind of music they like. It is much easier to talk about gender roles, norms, and sexism when we compare how Beyonce is discussed versus India.Arie or Jill Scott. Or the accolades that Eminem receives for his lyricism versus DMX or Tupac Shakur did for theirs. Or honestly, having students in the

Midwest discuss true country versus pop country and why one is better than the other as we discuss ageism, relationships, or socioeconomic status.

We encouraged people to answer three questions for themselves as they left our session:

1. Why does any of this matter? Why are we having these conversations?
2. Now that I know this "stuff," how do I integrate this into my everyday life (ecosystem)?
3. How do I have affirming conversations with my systems of influence?

We invite you to do the same because each answer will direct your next steps. Why would these conversations be important to your teaching or research? Are you having trouble recruiting or retraining talent? Then maybe you all need to figure out what you are not doing well enough to make your environment what you would ideally like it to be. One of the things that one of the authors does with her knowledge is to share it broadly. She will quantify this is what has worked for her but also encourage people to sort out how to adjust that knowledge for themselves. She will also recognize what she doesn't know and listen intently when others want to share knowledge with her. It would be a missed opportunity for us to say now that we never stop learning about areas within DEI. We learn what has been done and have to keep acquiring what is in progress or what moves the needle forward in best practice or care of these communities. Who do you take what you have learned to and use your realm of privilege to change the environment? The authors of this chapter, as Black women, do not have racial privilege but we have the benefit of education, stable health, and age in one case. We have to use those privileges while we have access to them and try to do as much as we can for others in those moments.

SO WHAT DO YOU DO NOW?

It seems trite to say that you should first figure out what you don't know but do that honestly. What communities are you lacking experience with? In what areas is your knowledge dated? Where can you go to learn more about both the historical and ongoing inequalities present in American society? Second, take time to read or learn from others. Reading is one of the easiest options and as long as we have public libraries it is one of the most affordable options. Reading about any of the following subjects would probably be highly enlightening:

- The dual consciousness that most minority groups in this country grow up developing and how the lack thereof for dominant group members hinders true understanding and conversations about race/racism and other forms of oppression. The term was originally coined by W. E. B. Du Bois (1903) but has been discussed by James Baldwin and others as well.
- Who J. Marion Sims is and how his "groundbreaking" work in advancing gynecological safety came at a horrifying cost.
- Why as a whole, most Americans are unaware of the struggles of minoritized communities.
- Historic mistrust between communities of color and law enforcement, the medical community, and sometimes between minoritized groups.

For personalized readings, we recommend the following books:

- *Lies My Teacher Told Me: Everything Your American History Textbook Got Wrong* by James Loewen
- *Beyond Your Bubble: How to Connect Across the Political Divide Skills and Strategies for Conversations that Work* by Tania Israel

For an in-depth and intriguing community read we recommend:

- *The Bluest Eye* by Toni Morrison
- *This Too Shall Pass* by E. Lynn Harris
- *The 1619 Project* by Nikole Hannah-Jones
- *The Art of Gathering* by Priya Parker
- *Inclusive Conversations* by Mary-Frances Winters
- *My Grandmother's Hands* by Resmaa Meankem

Finally, for those of you who want to read with your smaller children or just want to show them versions of themselves we recommend:

- *The Snowy Day* by Ezra Jack Keats
- *Happy to Be Nappy* by bell hooks
- *Hair Love* by Matthew Cherry
- *Please Baby Please* and *Please Puppy Please* by Spike and Tonya Lee
- *Sulwe* by Lupita Nyong'o

REFERENCES

Du Bois, W. E. B. (1903). *The Souls of Black Folks.* A. C. McClurg & Sons.
Goetz, D. (April 25, 2022). "'The world thinks the water crisis is over. It's not': Flint remembers 8 years since crisis began." *MLive.Com.*
Horton, B. A. (February 3, 2022). "'Ukrainians go first': How black and brown people are struggling to escape the Russian invasion." *EuroNews.*
Roberts-Miller, P. (December 11, 2019). "The deficit model of education and unintentional Racism." Patricia Roberts-Miller website. www.patriciarobertsmiller.com/2019/12/11/the-deficit-model-of-education-and-unintentional-racism/.

ACKNOWLEDGEMENT

I would like to thank Maqubè for her contributions to this chapter and the initial presentation. Her energy and willingness to dive into what is a controversial subject were the only way that we created something so phenomenal that we were asked to speak to another group on the same subject later. She greatly aided in the overall position we took to just be as open and honest as possible in our words, suggestions and deeds. She is sure to be a leader in the DEIJ space for years to come.

Chapter 7

Black Girl Magic Is Not Going to Kill Us

Rana Dotson and Rosalyn D. Davis

If you are a Black woman of a certain age, then you have likely heard the phrase Black Girl Magic. Not only have you heard it, but you would have felt it applied to you for something you have managed to do that your associates who lack melanin could not imagine having accomplished themselves. It is meant as a compliment. A testament to the strength of Black women everywhere. And maybe if another Black woman is lauding you, you may receive it as such, but let's just be clear. The magic comes at a price, and it is high time we stop paying it so freely. Almost six years ago, actor Jesse Williams broke the Blackosphere (Holland, 2007) by "preaching a word" during an award show acceptance speech. We'll be honest and say we didn't see it coming and were not fully prepared for Mr. Williams to fully encapsulate what we are about to tell you right now in one sentence. If you didn't see the speech, please give yourself a moment to find it so you can feel how the room shifted when he delivered the following words: "Just because we're magic, doesn't mean we're not real." After dropping that gold, he went on to discuss a number of issues crucial to the Black community and our ability to breathe and exist in the United States. What we are going to delve into, specifically, is the toll this "magic" has on Black women.

    A number of Black women are struggling right now under the weight of expectation. We are somehow meant to work longer and harder than our co-workers, and when we acknowledge a moment of weakness people start to wonder if we are falling apart. They don't look at the demands the system has placed on us without relief or support in lots of cases. We are hired for the wins and then we make things happen. We are sometimes abandoned when our bodies are too stressed out to let us sleep, eat, or work at both the paid and unpaid labor each of us routinely performs. If we slack on the home front it seems to be noticed more and we catch judgment from those who look like us just as fast as from those who do not. For some reason, Black women are just expected to make do with less of everything, without asking for support or needing a break. That expectation damages our health and well-being and shortens our lives. And that is fundamentally unfair. Nearly every woman in this collection has had a health scare at some point. One in which we had to reassess our priorities, turn down things of interests, acknowledge that our bodies needed a rest, and wonder what we might be giving up in the process.

That may sound defeatist, but the truth is we very rarely are given a seat at the proverbial tables of power or put in places where the Powers that Be can hear us and try to impart change. The authors of this chapter were both delayed by health challenges at different times and struggled with what it meant to be waylaid by demands our bodies could not meet. The frustration in knowing why is not lessened by the reality of the situation and, if anything, just provides another reminder that we aren't meeting someone's expectations. And by "someone" we sometimes mean "ourselves"—the saddest part now is in knowing we have internalized the pressure and the expectations are sometimes self-imposed. However, one of the highlights of Black womanhood is having a sister come lift you when you are unable to do so yourself. As we spoke about this chapter and its development, something became evident. Even when the body is weak, the mind is still sharp and ready to tackle the world.

The lead author has been struggling with her health for an extended period of time. However, over that time I have continued to support my family and tried to maintain a connection with my place of employment. I checked in with my co-author repeatedly and relayed regrets about missing the deadlines that had been set. What I primarily did though in doing so was reminding us all to extend each other grace, which if we were paying attention to ourselves would mean extending grace for our own struggles. I am an accomplished professional. I have been appointed to boards nationally and asked to consult on projects due to my experience and expertise. I have done phenomenal things professionally, all while supporting my husband and family in their own growth and development. These moments when my body is not totally under my control are foreign to me and would be to most Black women. If there's nothing else we can do, it's to make a way out of no way. You've heard it in music, movies, and books before. The mythical Black woman who fed her family when she had almost no money left from her underpaid job. The exceptional Black woman who managed to succeed despite not having the same support systems in place that bolstered her white counterparts. The overachieving Black woman who dominates some profession for so long that her eventual decline to normal performance levels is met with derision.

What you don't hear is the moments in which all of those women have to cry silently and wonder who is going to be strong for them when they need to be weak.

The second author of this chapter has been a caregiver for a parent for an extended period of time. It is a role that women have played for their family members for generations so in that case there's nothing terribly exciting about that statement. The problem really is that it started at least ten years ahead of schedule and I still had to finish a degree, find a job, relocate, and establish multi-pronged care for the parent. I was lucky compared to others in my family, though. My profession would more than likely allow me to comfortably support the two of them without struggling most of the time. However, it would impact my ability to change jobs easily, travel, marry, and socialize for quite some time. There was no time left to really do any of those things while I was maintaining my responsibilities at work and home without screaming into the void. It took an intervention to remind me that I had to take care of myself so that I might be around long enough to enjoy the time I had with my mother and my work.

We started there for a reason. We are not exceptions to the rule. We are clear examples of what is asked of Black women all over the country. If we're being honest, it's happening all over the globe and the stress is enough to kill us if we are not careful. There is no protection, no padding, for us just because we are educated or in high-paying jobs. Both Venus and Serena Williams have had health issues that may have killed other women without their resources. Venus has dealt with an autoimmune disorder for quite some time that has altered her professional career because it can exhaust her to even get out of bed. Serena has a blood clotting disorder that has to be medicated in order to make sure one doesn't arbitrarily kill her. A disorder that she couldn't be medicated for when she was pregnant with her daughter and that almost did kill her post-birth because the medical staff didn't listen to her when she said that her body wasn't feeling right (Williams, 2018). Had her husband not intervened we may have lost one of the greatest female athletes of our time because medical professionals thought she was just paranoid (Williams, 2018).

Just as they thought Dr. Susan Moore (Andone, 2020), a physician, was paranoid and intimidating to the medical staff when she presented with milder symptoms of COVID-19. She knew she was not well and said so repeatedly and firmly, but instead of having medical professionals take her seriously (in the hospital system in which she was employed, to boot), she was sent home. She had enough wherewithal to go to a different hospital, where she was admitted, but it was too late. She died within a few weeks. This was not an isolated experience, unfortunately. Several Black women and men were denied basic care at the height of the pandemic or were forced to keep working in frontline positions that exposed them to the deadly virus and prematurely ended their lives. This was true for other communities of color as well. In many cases, these BIPOC individuals, as frontline workers, were also initially blamed for their contracting the disease. They heard variations of "if they had just taken better care of themselves and not had all of those pre-existing conditions then the death toll would have been lower." That honestly terrified the second author who has several of those pre-existing conditions and feared for who would take care of my mother should I get ill. I didn't take the time to figure out who would take care of me if I was sick because the answer more than likely would be no one. My only sibling and his wife live hundreds of miles away and have two minor children to care for themselves. Even if my brother could get to me, he also has a pre-existing medical condition that requires weighing the health risk for everyone. Every day I just had to keep my fingers crossed, hope for the best, and be thankful that my career was one that could be maintained from home.

As the world has slowly tried to correct itself during the last two years, Black women have started looking for ways to implement Black Girl Magic for their own benefit. More Black women are quitting jobs that do not nurture them. They are traveling and meditating and exercising and gathering together and working out and going to therapy and, most of all, just stopping to breathe. Collectively, it is as if Black womanhood finally said enough. It's not enough to just survive and obtain another badge of honor. Recognition is good but a good night's sleep is so much better.

BLACK WARRIORS NEED A RETREAT (TOO): THIS IS A DREAM FOR RESTFUL, REFLECTIVE HEALING RETREAT FOR BLACK WOMEN ON THE GROWING EDGE

We are thought leaders, practitioners dedicated to the health, safety, advancement, and overall well-being of Black people and our communities. We deserve to be unapologetically cared for. We deserve the resources for repair. Before we continue, the lead author wants to share a personal narrative about why Black women resting needs to be understood, encouraged, supported, and celebrated. You will read about the phone call that altered her life and why writing this chapter was both deeply personal and important for her.

I answered the phone—it was the rheumatologist. I had ended up there after a winding turn of events beginning with the dents in her legs, the ever-present tenderness and ache in every place bones connected to bone, muscle, and tissue, the funny fluttering sensations in my chest. The primary care doctor looked at her list of scattershot symptoms, which had been carefully kept on a notepad app on my phone. I had managed to lift my head above the whooshing fog of work, home, and school grind to notice my body in glimpses. To take furtive notes between chores, on bathroom breaks, or upon lying down in the evening.

> "Your test results came back consistent with Mixed Connective Tissue Disease."

> My fluttering heart seemed to skip two extra beats. Had I understood correctly? Wait, Mixed, what? Slow down.

> "What is it again? Mixed . . . "

> "Mixed . . . Connective . . . Tissue . . . Disease. It's rare but we can treat you. We will get you in for your follow-up appointment where I can answer all your questions, but I wanted to let you know the results right away."

> "Okay . . . " (shallow, tight breathing). "Thank you."

> Click.

I had no idea then what was to come over the next year would fundamentally unravel everything I knew about my relationship with my body and my work. But Congresswoman Ayanna Pressley's raw honesty revealing her journey seared itself into my mind. I benefited from her courage. Her courage is the reason I'm telling my story today.

On Being the Problem

> We accompany work of activism and justice by equipping for reflection, resilience, and repair.
>
> —Tippet, 2022

Black women need a retreat. As the public conscious became reattuned to the Black Lives Matter movement, Congresswoman Pressley's body became a billboard for the effects of embodied toxic stress (Kennedy, 2020). Her story entered the historical ledger, joining a long succession of Black bodies manifesting the same. Congresswoman Pressley's hair fell out over a period of months, hidden in plain view, while she continued appearing on television, working in the Capitol building, and showing up for the people. All the while, her balding head was covered by hair extensions and wigs. To the casual observer, her changed look appeared to be the whimsy of creative hair expression. Yet her expensive wigs masked a sobering reality: the last of her hair fell out the night before the House voted on articles of impeachment against former president Donald Trump.

Congresswoman Pressley's journey is personal to her, yet familiar to so many of us. It resonates within our collective Black story: we pay with our bodies for the work we do, showing up daily to carry, not only ourselves, but others, all while carrying the load of anti-Black racism (Thomas et al., 2011). How? Through centuries of conditioning. For hundreds of years, our ancestors were forced to override their bodies' signals of distress, pain, and illness. We were forced to "push through" during slavery, even when that pushing through meant being driven to one's death (Thomas et al., 2011). When chattel slavery ended, our collective survival required pushing through. Pushing through became synonymous with Black identity—it was passed down intergenerationally (Thomas et al., 2011). It became a virtue: a legacy of brutal enslavement intermingled with the puritanical. This thorny vine has been choking our communities, killing us as an epidemic of chronic illnesses afflicts our bodies at many times the rate of white bodies in the United States (Thomas et al., 2011).

Congresswoman Pressley's journey is symbolic in its archetypal reflection of what it actually means to be Black, vulnerable, and strong. In her courage to share her journey and "reveal" her bald head, polished by alopecia, we see our own collective wounds, our vulnerability and strength. We see our resolve to say "yes, and so what" in the face of our challenges. Our tendency to see and acknowledge great ugly truths while maintaining our own sense of grounded hope and faith is a central tenet of Black warriorship, resistance, and resilience. Our rootedness allows us to bend and not be destroyed, even under the high winds of racism, or the high pressure demands of being the "Black leader" in the room, while also maintaining the normal rhythms of our daily lives for ourselves and our families. Yet, the high winds take their toll. And none of our bodies are immune to the effects of racism and the inability to make mistakes publicly.

Let's talk about two specific public moments with Black women in the public eye over the last year. The first is involving Simone Biles, an accomplished, highly decorated gymnast who had publicly disclosed her sexual assault at the hands of a team doctor all while destroying records. She was the unparalleled leader of the women's team and with that came the expectations of an entire country. She had already brought immense acclaim to the United States with her previous performances, but when she couldn't perform skills that are named for her, and that other athletes do not dare to attempt, she was labeled a quitter (Rose & MacKenzie, 2021). Very few people understood and acknowledged the potential physical danger in her trying to perform while battling the "twisties," as it is termed; most people overlooked that the team still won a gold medal without her participation (Goldman, 2021). Some may excuse the vocal and critical outcry because it was the Olympics and people get overly invested in the Olympics. That may be true, and the masses are quick to jump on anyone who doesn't perform the way they would like, but the reward is not commensurate to the stress carried at the expense of Black bodies, Black women in particular. More recently, as we were working to complete this chapter in fact, someone we'll discuss more later ended up in the spotlight. Lizzo is a Black woman who is a skilled flautist, singer, and rapper. She has made some very engaging music and during lockdown became a bit of a social media star often lauded for her "realness" and humor. In this era of social media presence, artists interact much more with their fanbase than ever before, and that may have been why so many of them felt entitled to direct their ire at Lizzo over one word in a recently released song. For the sake of this work, we won't repeat it in these pages lest we are accused of the same bias regarding persons with disabilities, but it was a word that had a well-established slang definition within the Black community. That definition, essentially, is on par with someone acting out of character because they were provoked or triggered. Lizzo was reviled for choosing this word without regard for the duality of its meaning in the Black community. Twitter activists launched an assault that continued until Lizzo released a public statement and rereleased her song without the word being utilized (Rajkumar, 2022). Now, the grandmothers among us may have said "she's better than me," meaning they would not have apologized or honestly cared that people were upset. The fact that more problematic lyrics are clearly present across a variety of artists did not appear to matter to the protestors, nor were they held to the same expectation for better behavior. This protest was just for our girl, the musical multi-hyphenate, Lizzo—a woman who dares to put herself fully, freely, in the public eye.

> All around us life is dying and life is being born. The fruit ripens on the tree, the roots are silently at work in the darkness of the earth against a time when there shall be new leaves, fresh blossoms, green fruit. Such is the growing edge! This is the basis of hope in moments of despair, the incentive to carry on when times are out of joint and dreams whiten into ash. The birth of the child—life's most dramatic answer to death—this is the growing edge incarnate. Look well to the growing edge! (Thurman, 2014, p. 174)

The late Black civil rights leader Howard Thurman's words "look well to the growing edge" (2014) inspired Parker J. Palmer (Newcomer & Palmer, n.d.), renowned author, educator, and activist who focuses on issues in education, community, leadership, spirituality, and social change, to ask, "What's your growing edge?" Growing edge callings demand that we exist in two elements at all times—earth and air. Suspended between heaven and earth, navigating hope and sorrow—this liminal space is our home; and from this place of creative tension, we as Black leaders produce our most startling gifts to humanity. We have a particular challenge in creating our own inner unity: as Black people in a society built by the ancestors' blood, the paradox of existing within the water of white supremacy leads every Black child to develop what W. E. B. Du Bois called "double consciousnesses" (Du Bois, 1903).

This brilliant process of inner fragmentation experienced by every Black child is a subconscious attempt to protect ourselves from the effects of white supremacy. This transformational coping response to the trauma of racism occurs as the Black child loses racial innocence. Our rite of passage into maturity and wholeness, what Du Bois (1903) refers to as "self-conscious manhood," begins when we grow into our full ownership of self, reclaiming the fullness of our identities as human beings, beginning the process of healing this inner division and wound. The problem? This inner healing process is constantly disrupted by the ongoing trauma of living in a racist society. Even in places of supposed respite, Black people must contend with white supremacy. In conferences, leadership development programs, empowerment programs, and retreats, we often show up as the only one in the room and are forced to wade through the heavy waters of processing others' grief at the Black experience. Black women need a retreat—especially our black leaders and warriors—to give space and rest to recover from the toxic and grinding effects of navigating liminal spaces with open wounds. We also need a place to celebrate who we are, how we have led, and the wisdom generated from our personal and collective experiences. In short, a place to sit in the joy of our human skin without reserve.

There is something uniquely wonderful about being in fellowship with a group of Black women. That can be something as simple as a dinner once a month to something as elaborate as the retreats that are sponsored by a growing number of Black women across the globe. They deliberately create time and space for Black women to gather with each other and just bask in our melanin. Retreat companies like the Imara Retreat, OmNoire, Liesano Living, and Africa With Us offer Black women the opportunity and ability to decompress, focus on their health and wellness, as well as journey from their homebases that tend to expect the herculean efforts we need to step back from us if we are seen as slightly available (Turner-Ewert, 2022). These may not be accessible to every Black woman for a variety of factors so we encourage you to find the space you need to decompress and stand firm in your self-care. The second author is a huge proponent of monthly visits to whatever makes you feel better and you can afford. I highly advocate massages and letting someone else perform my loc maintenance. It is definitely something I could do but that four hours, and scalp massage, lets me just breathe and allows my arms to not hate me at the end of a weekend.

REST, RELATE, RELEASE

You have read stories from our colleagues about the stressors that inundate Black womanhood. While we have slowly begun to embrace the need for self-care and what it means if we do not take that time for ourselves, we still need the space to do that. That sometimes means that we need to be alone to fellowship with each other because that is when we will recharge and find our way forward again. Sometimes that may mean having uncomfortable conversations with our allies and friends because to not do so would either allow ourselves or others to be harmed. At other times that may mean we just disengage for our own protection and sit still in the emotions we are struggling with in that moment. In spite of the fact that Black women are one of the most educated groups of people in the United States, we are still confronted with stereotypes and tropes about us that are damaging. People loved Oprah Winfrey when she first emerged the same way they love Lizzo now. You know they have nothing in common but their weight and the appearance that they are affable and accessible. I (Rosalyn) have heard and read of white women in particular calling Lizzo their "spirit animal." It is meant as a compliment, I'm sure, but it reads as demeaning. If there was an off switch for the misogynoir, Black women would flip it as often as possible to the off position.

While we recognize that we are centuries past slavery and acknowledge the progress we have made, we draw wisdom from the model that was developed by enslaved people working with abolitionists during this painful epoch in our history. The lessons point to a deeper way of connecting, strategizing, and mobilizing resources. They highlight for us the fact that "ally-ship" is a necessary, but not a sufficient, condition for progress toward full healing and freedom within the Black community. Black people continue to engage in a freedom struggle that includes our continuous journey toward deep collective and individual healing.

Conductors Needed

What is a conductor? Araminta "Minty" Ross aka Harriet Tubman was the most well-known conductor in this deep network of enslaved and freed black people and white abolitionists (Michaels, 2015). She made her way north with a vision, following the voice of God. Alliances were complex—some Black people were convinced to work against others' freedom in order to preserve themselves. Trusting the wrong white person would have meant her certain, swift death along with all those whom she was aiding. But white conductors along the Underground Railroad were essential to the plan to reach freedom. These conductors were willing to risk life, limb, and property to support the plans and vision that Harriet Tubman had to get her people to freedom. They were willing to make themselves vulnerable, just as the enslaved people they were helping were in a constant state of vulnerability. They were willing to follow Harriet's lead as she followed the correct path led by her own intuition, intelligence, experience, and spiritual guidance. These conductors chose to be vulnerable and pledged their physical and financial support in the process. They serve as a model for what is needed today: modern-day conductors, new age Harriets.

Our modern-day conductors need to be willing to supply the resources for Black women, and other Black, Indigenous, people of color (BIPOC), to be able to comfortably rest and reset. Whether providing finances, meeting space, session facilitators, supplies, or treatment opportunities, recognize that all of it is needed and should be defended when people ask why that offset is there. There is a risk to doing this, of course, and Black women know that more than others. However, through a number of metrics that the United States likes to measure, we know that if Black women are allowed and supported in their efforts to succeed and be healthy that everyone benefits (Bofino et al., 2021). These conductors need to check in with the Black women they are trying to serve, assure they are not ignoring the talent and cultural capital within the community, and to make sure that the services provided are culturally appropriate and not operating from a deficit model (Roberts-Miller, 2019). They also need to be willing to hear when they have overstepped or misunderstood or are adding to the stressors of the very people they are trying to help. You may have seen a quote from author Robert S. Jones Jr. (2015) that is often misattributed to James Baldwin: "We can disagree and still love each other unless your disagreement is rooted in my oppression and denial of my humanity and right to exist." Listen to Black women if we tell you that a mistake was made, and do what you can to work in community without excluding their voices from whatever you choose to provide for them. It is hard to adjust from the old ways of doing things, but if you cannot then ultimately you will likely cause harm, even if it is unintended harm.

North Star Guides Needed

Tubman led and worked through a network of freed and enslaved Black people who also leveraged their resources, life, and limb to ensure that those who had embarked on the road to freedom reached the goal. Many freed Black people were conductors along the way, and they worked closely with white abolitionists. Some freed Black people leveraged substantial wealth, but most used whatever they possessed, whether it was wit or wealth. It will take all of us working together to get the retreat we all need. This means that the work that we do sometimes must be in house and leading as an example to others. The self-love, support, and community building sometimes have to be "in-house" activities. We have to encourage each other to rest and recover, because without it we cannot release the stress and ongoing trauma that is experienced on the individual and collective level. Some of us will have more ability than others to do this, either because we have the resources, know where to find them, or have some level of public cache that allows us to reach others more easily. If you, like us, are one of those folks, please be aware that we are in a unique position to do good things and we cannot abuse that privilege. We also need to acknowledge when we are not the best people to do the work that is being asked of us in that moment. That's difficult, especially for Black women who are used to being able to make miracles occur (Black Girl Magic), but in our efforts to lead others we must also recognize when we aren't able to be out front on any particular effort.

We have watched, with no small amount of admiration, the Wade family wade into precarious territory in support of their daughter. Retired professional basketball player Dwayne Wade and his wife Gabrielle Union, an actress, a Black couple, have been vocal about supporting their daughter Zaya, who came out publicly as transgender several years ago. People have accused them of having an agenda and allowing everything from Hollywood to their wealth confuse their child (Aniftos, 2020). While the attackers have been clear about the ways in which they think the Wades' unconditional love for their child is harmful to the community, they have not considered what it means to the lonely or abandoned Black trans kids to see public figures so wholeheartedly loving a member of their family. The derision doesn't take into account the Black parents who may be struggling with their own feelings about their LGBTQ+ children and who need to see someone else unapologetically loving and accepting someone they care about. The deep sighs and feelings of understanding that may be generated by this family will have ripples we cannot understand. Just in the same way that hatred, lies, and mistrust have created ripples; we are still struggling to rid ourselves of them before they overwhelm us.

CONCLUSION

You have read our suggestions throughout the chapter so we will not summarize them here. What we will do in conclusion is reiterate that Black women deserve everything we have encouraged them to seek and you to potentially provide them. It is troubling the number of times and ways in which "womanhood" seems to exclude Black women and other women of color. The ways in which womanhood is practiced seemingly devalues Black women's bodies, intelligence, contributions, and their safety. Until a more expansive option or definition exists, then books like this will be a necessary work to explore instead of a description of what used to be that we finally took care of and eradicated. We just gave you a long description of what Black women are asking for when we discuss intersectionality and what it is we really need from allies and friends (Crenshaw, 1989). Your Black woman work friend probably needs to be supported in her efforts or highly encouraged to take a vacation. Your Black female client maybe needs to be encouraged to slow down and get help finding assistance for the caretaking she is tasked with. The Black mother in your child's play group could probably use a spa day as much as you do—invite her next time. Do what you can to encourage the Black women in your life to take care of themselves. Do what you can to support that self-care. Do what you need to, Black women, to recognize when you need to put yourself first, and most of all shed the guilt that is inherently involved when we do. If you aren't okay, no one else will be. We know that; we need to live it.

REFERENCES

Andone, D. (December 25, 2020). "A Black doctor died of Covid-19 weeks after accusing hospital staff of racist treatment." *CNN.com*. www.cnn.com/2020/12/24/us/black-doctor-susan-moore-covid-19/index.html.

Aniftos, R. (February 18, 2020). "Young Thug slams Dwyane Wade, misgenders his daughter Zaya." *Blllboard.com*. www.billboard.com/music/rb-hip-hop/young-thug-dwyane-wade-daughter-zaya-8551352/.

Bofino, B. A., Zafar, R., Maguire, J., & Mintz, M. (June 8, 2021). "How the advancement of Black Women will build a better economy for all." www.spglobal.com/en/research-insights/featured/how-the-advancement-of-black-women-will-build-a-better-economy-for-all.

Crenshaw, K. (1989). Demarginalizing the intersection of race and sex: A Black feminist critique of antidiscrimination doctrine, feminist theory and antiracist politics. The University of Chicago Legal Forum 140: 139–167.

Du Bois, W. E. B., (1903). *The Souls of Black Folks.* A. C. McClurg & Sons.

Goldman, T. (July 29, 2021). "Simone Biles got the 'Twisties' at the Tokyo Olympics. Here's what that means." www.npr.org/sections/tokyo-olympics-live-updates/2021/07/29/1022151827/simone-biles-got-the-twisties-at-the-tokyo-olympics-heres-what-that-means.

Holland, F. (2007). "An essay on AfroSpear nomenclature: What we call ourselves and why." Francis Hollander blog. francislholland.blogspot.com/2007/06/essay-of-afrospear-nomenclature-what-is.html.

Jones Jr., R. S. [@sonofbaldwin]. (August 18, 2015). We can disagree and still love each other unless your disagreement is rooted in my oppression and denial of my humanity and right to exist, and [Tweet]. Twitter. twitter.com/SonofBaldwin/status/633644373423562753.

Kennedy, M. (January 17, 2020). "'Freed from the secret': Rep. Ayanna Pressley opens up about living with alopecia." *NPR.org.* www.npr.org/2020/01/17/797295985/freed-from-the-secret-rep-ayanna-pressley-opens-up-about-living-with-alopecia.

Michaels, D. (2015). "Harriet Tubman." *National Women's History Museum.* www.womenshistory.org/education-resources/biographies/harriet-tubman.

Newcomer, C., and Palmer, P. (n.d.). The Growing Edge collaboration. www.newcomerpalmer.com/.

Rajkumar, S. (June 14, 2022). "Lizzo rerecords 'Grrrls' following criticism over ableist lyric." www.npr.org/2022/06/14/1104925003/lizzo-rerecords-grrrls-criticism-ableism.

Roberts-Miller, P. (December 11, 2019). "The deficit model of education and unintentional racism." Patricia Roberts-Miller website. www.patriciarobertsmiller.com/2019/12/11/the-deficit-model-of-education-and-unintentional-racism/.

Rose, C., & MacKenzie, M. (August 3, 2021). "Olympics 2021: Simone Biles pulls out of the gymnastics all-around final." *Glamour.* www.glamour.com/story/olympics-2021-simone-biles-has-pulled-out-of-the-gymnastics-team-final.

Thomas, S. B., Quinn, S. C., Butler, J., Fryer, C. S., & Garza, M. A. (2011). Toward a fourth generation of disparities research to achieve health equity. *Annual Review of Public Health, 32,* 399.416.

Thurman, H. (2014). *The Growing Edge.* Friends United Press.

Tippet, K. (2022). The On Being Project. onbeing.org/.

Turner-Ewert, C. (2022). "Six amazing Black-owned wellness retreats making a difference." *Vacayou.com* vacayou.com/magazine/black-owned-wellness-retreats/.

Williams, S. (February 20, 2018). "What my life-threatening experience taught me about giving birth." *CNN.com.* www.cnn.com/2018/02/20/opinions/protect-mother-pregnancy-williams-opinion/index.html.

Chapter 8

Please Tell Us How to Fix the Problem of the Problematic Women of Color

Rosalyn D. Davis

This chapter could have just as easily been called Protect Black Women or Support Black Women but that is too simple for what we need to discuss. One of the most intriguing parts about being a woman of color in the workforce is observing the number of times and ways in which you are asked for your expertise. Sometimes it is a random email from a total stranger asking to pick your brain, without compensation. Other times it is meeting with a student or junior colleague who has been directed to you for no other apparent reason than you both are from the same racial/ethnic background. Still others, it may be that we identify an issue and hope that by highlighting it we can address it quickly. Most often though, for myself anyway, it is being hired specifically to address issues that the agency/site/employer is having and seems unable to address on their own. I mentioned in chapter 3 that in general I'm okay with that because I know where we stand and what my expectations are in that given role. What I have not been entirely prepared for is the number of times that the solution is ignored or in the process of addressing the situation a much more glaring problem arises. The frustration, annoyance, and feelings of defeat are palpable when that happens, and I have typically not been in a position to unilaterally address what needs to be done to take care of the entire problem.

WHEN AND WHERE I ENTER

If you have looked into any diversity, equity, and inclusion work over the last decade then you will have either (1) noticed a particular pattern or (2) seen a flow chart detailing the problematic woman of color in an organization. I don't want to just drop the image within these pages without having a rich conversation to accompany it so bear with me. A woman of color will find it more difficult than her counterparts to even be invited into the spaces where leadership opportunities may be doled out. However, before she even arrives there are barriers. We know that names that appear to be more ethnic than others can hinder hiring opportunities even when the candidate is highly qualified (Bertrand & Mullainathan, 2003; Kline et al., 2021). My name does not block me from opportunities, but if people knew more about Black culture at a glance then I would likely be in the same boat as Lakisha and Jamal were in the previous studies. Looking at my curriculum vitae, someone who knew about Black culture would quickly note that I attended a Historically Black College or University (HBCU), am a member of a historically Black sorority (part of the colloquially named Divine 9 Black Greek Lettered organizations) and perform a plethora of volunteer activities that support the Black community in particular. You may also see attendance at a Hispanic Serving Institution as well and may assume that I was Latina as a former colleague did. Rosalyn could be a shortened version of similarly sounding Latina names I guess. Regardless, if people knew more about nonwhite culture, it is reasonable to assume that even if my name didn't trip me up then my other personal activities would. Thankfully, they don't otherwise I wouldn't be in a position to even write this chapter. My research being tied to Black culture or my professional activities focusing on diversity allow whomever people assume I am to be invited into the spaces where I can at least discuss what is needed from the future star employee who is hired.

My interviews have been intriguing as well. Prior to the late 2000s, it wasn't common that a photo of me was publicly available for anyone looking to see who I was before I interviewed. The benefit of growing up before there was rampant internet usage. I mention this for one reason. When interviewers want to give a very homey welcome to candidates, they often pick us up from the airport or meet us for dinner the night before we have the full interview day. Great, it's nice to see how people interact with you when it is not a fully professional moment and you do not have to go hunting for food. However, each of these meetings before you could find me online led to a moment of me being able to quietly observe the person appointed to pick me up because as I came out of a hotel room or off an airplane, they were not looking for a short Black woman. One of my point people raised his eyebrows hopefully at several women as they walked ahead of me but started to look at his phone as I got closer. I didn't take it personally because I really needed to use the bathroom. So, after I did that and got my luggage, I made my way back to him. He was pleasant and I really did enjoy our conversation. However, if I had opted to be difficult, I could have waited a bit longer or headed on over to catch a cab. So I have unlocked the first rung of getting access but once there the microaggressions and invasive questions are plentiful.

   I won't regale you with stories about each interview, but one is endemic of what I referred to at the end of the previous paragraph. I won't give you a time frame so as to not potentially out the employer, but let's just say it started off rocky and sped downhill with skis that were on fire and an avalanche chasing those skis. Dinner at a restaurant that is great for a romantic dinner but not as much for a lightweight interview dinner with two potential colleagues including the only other person of color on staff. I note that for two reasons. The first being the person of color is almost always on a search committee when there's an opening regardless of if they want to or should be. The second being the only point of commonality we had was that were nonwhite women. She wasn't hostile but she wasn't friendly either. We spent most of the dinner focused on aspects of my dissertation that she appeared to disagree with and wanted more feedback on before I was hired apparently. This went on for three hours before she finally relented and said that she had done something similar and really just wanted to hear me explain my positions. When I returned to the hotel, slightly hungry and a bit annoyed, I realized my room had only been paid for one evening and I would need to check out before I left in the morning. Then the interview day began during which I met with one Black professional who kept trying to convince me it was a great place to work even though he had left several times only to be recruited back, others didn't seem to know who they were meeting with or what I would be doing, I was asked to take my cute pumps on a fifteen-minute stroll from our primary location to have lunch because they do it all the time, had to answer questions from a specific theoretical orientation that I was specifically asked to not address, and when I met with the person who would ultimately be my boss was told they weren't sure how they would evaluate me because aspects of my position were not what they were used to and gaslit about the salary. What I took from that experience was that even if they don't know who I am before I arrive that once I do it was fair game to attempt to pick apart until I proved I was worthy of their time and energy. What they ended up taking from that experience was my disinterest in the position and tires nearly leaving burn marks on the street as I fled away from them. You may wonder what microaggressions I saw over the day and a half I was with them, and I am happy to explain that to you.

First, they hadn't considered that a Black woman was the doctor they were looking for to start the dinner process. Then the next morning no one had actually taken the time to read my materials before they arrived or ask how to pronounce my name before they butchered it routinely. The walk to lunch may seem innocuous but no one asked if I had any mobility issues or if I had any allergies to the only cuisine on the menu. Throughout the day it was clear that previous Black employees in this unit began looking for a new job within months of them arriving because none had been there longer than a year before departing. This group did almost no work on DEI issues and had not considered how to work with individuals who were low income or struggling to pay for our services. Finally, instead of seeing my potential hire as a moment to diversify the group and add services they were not offering, there was a concerted effort to hire me as cheaply as possible and mold me into clone of everyone else there. It felt like a tremendous waste of time and quite frankly was insulting. It reminds me now of the lawsuit that Brian Flores has filed against the National Football League for having what amounts to pointless interviews to meet the diversity hiring requirements (Jackson, 2022). I don't know who they hired instead of me because honestly I never looked, but I am eternally gratefully that I had other opportunities available to me in that moment instead of potentially being stuck in an environment that was neither receptive to nor supportive of what I could bring to the table. My story isn't terribly unique and represents the first roadblock to having women of color, Black women, involved in repairing the broken things in our work settings.

FINDING A SEAT AT THE TABLE

Once we make it past the interview stage and are allowed to enter the spaces that are not built for us, we have to decide which version of us will be present at work. You've read a lot about Du Bois (1903) and double consciousness, but there is another aspect of this that can influence who is invited to the table and what we are allowed to do when there. Several years ago, I was giving a training to the leadership on my campus related to microaggressions. This was in direct response to us losing several minoritized and female colleagues because of things that were done or said to them. Once we got past the bit of resistance that was present, we had a great conversation. So much so that we didn't need about ten minutes of time because we hadn't had to fight to get a point across to the group. It must have just been kismet in that moment, but I decided to share with the group some things that were not part of the workshop but that made it difficult for the Black women in the room to be fully present all day every day. Hang on to your hats dear readers because you may have heard this before and never considered it. Or you may have never heard it and will be shocked. Black women in traditionally white spaces have to be bilingual. Not in the traditional sense even though that would be nice. No, Black women have to be able to code switch without missing a beat (Spencer et al., 2022; Apugo, 2019; Culver, 2018). It's not that we are speaking an entirely new language, but we have to be able to convey information in a way that is receptive to our audiences or risk exclusion from decision-making positions (Spencer et al., 2022; Apugo, 2019; Culver, 2018). For the sake of transparency, and because I didn't want to put any of the other Black women in the room on the spot, I shared with the group that I am used to being very direct with my colleagues of color and especially in personal circles with Black women. However, I discovered that in dealing with colleagues from the dominant culture group that I cannot do that without someone assuming I am upset, rude, or something else that reads negatively. If I can convey my thoughts in six words, that is what I would prefer but through many examples I have learned that I needed to use at least ten more words that don't enhance the six-word message unless I want to be misinterpreted. I finally shared with them how exhausting that was to experience each day and was met by deep sighs and agreements from the few Black women who were there. The shock that rippled across the room should not have been surprising but when the default is how you communicate there is a delay in understanding what that means for other groups. There are Black women and others from minoritized groups who refuse to code switch because it is so exhausting, demeaning, and unnecessary, but the system we are working to disengage from problematic practices is slow to adjust. I have to use my Dr. Davis voice to accomplish things that Rosalyn should be able to do just as easily. I have been encouraged to watch my tone when another colleague was poking the proverbial bear and I had not been on a public disparagement tour of said colleague. And I have had to begin meeting actively with other Black women away from the seats afforded to us by those in power so each of us can breathe and be free.

The table isn't really shared if different members assembled around it are not free to be themselves without a loss of respect, status, or ability to impart change (Spencer et al., 2022). Before I can reasonably recruit new faces to the table, I need to know that we are aware of the problem and are committed to changing it before we continue down broken pathways. I also need to know that those faces will not just be there for window dressing. Diversifying those gathered without empowering them with the resources, time, or power that they need to directly address problematic situations only leads to frustration for everyone involved. In Miller's (2020) piece on what happens when Black employees take on DEI work for their organizations, one person directly speaks to this issue. Ms. Crowder shares that "They are often not protected and don't have the power to make changes" (Miller, 2020). Do not just promote them to the table because they are Black or because they offer to join with everyone else. Make sure they are afforded what they need to advance an agenda and to genuinely improve things for everyone else in the organization (Rendon, 2021). That means placing them in the power structure with assigned duties, expectations, and the power to implement change instead of just being the newly titled person or the go to diversity expert. They should legitimately be experts as well and not just someone with a presumed diverse background (Miller, 2020). Well-trained folks will help you move forward. Also consider that diversity expertise does not preclude expertise in other areas. Unless you hired someone in a DEI specified role, do not ignore the skills they accumulated outside of the DEI arena (Bui, 2019; Rendon, 2021). Arbitrarily chosen people will help with your numbers but will more than likely ensure that you just stagnate where there could be growth. Those folks will also cause no shortage of frustration for your diverse employees or community. Seeing individuals maintain the status quo or who cannot relate to the communities they purport to serve does not help reassure diverse constituents that you are committed to being good diversity advocates.

KNOCK THE TABLE OVER

Very rarely will there be enough time to just get comfortable at the table and hope for the best. Once you accomplish one goal, the stakes will be raised along with the expectations on what could be done. A colleague and I have been sharing our DEI wins within a circle of like-minded individuals. It all sounds very impressive but each of us has been working at this avalanche of wins for more than five years and it took each of us finally saying enough to get there. We have gone from a loosely attended group of diversity trainings that were optional to having a mandatory training requirement for faculty over the course of a few years. Both of us had been asking about such a requirement since we arrived on campus but were told repeatedly that it could not happen in the way we were hoping. I had a seat at the table so I could keep asking about it, but I couldn't push the needle in the position I was inhabiting. Neither could she or the two of us together. We didn't have the strength in numbers to impart change (Rendon, 2021). It took another group approaching both of us about our thoughts on such a requirement, and each of us sharing anecdotal evidence about colleagues and students who had either left our campus or felt discriminated against by one of our colleagues. Because of my role, I could also tell them very pointedly that because of some of their employees or leadership I could not recruit for different portions of the organization. Diverse communities are not as disconnected as one might hope and if one of us has a bad experience with someone then it may come up as people ask about living or working in a new community. I know there are portions of my home state that I would never live in, and I know there are only a limited number of places and positions I would take in my current state. However, we wanted to make sure that voices were heard so we hosted a series of listening sessions about the training requirement and were able to share that information back to the decision makers. The vote wasn't unanimous, but it passed by a healthy margin. That was achieved after we revamped our general education and program learning objectives to make sure that every student is touched by global and specific diversity content, launched a center for our minoritized and diverse communities, started a series of town halls on issues impacting diverse and minoritized communities, launched well-attended trainings to help us become more supportive to our growing LGBTQ+ population, and committed to a series of mentoring initiatives. We know there is an immense amount of work that is still to be done but to others we have achieved the impossible because they are still assembling the table and gathering the invitation list.

Instead of taking a deep sigh and hoping that forward momentum will continue we will rest this summer because we need to recharge and then start planning for the next wave of what must be done. How can we use the most recent wins to recruit new individuals to campus? What can we do to make sure that our current diverse and minoritized communities feel welcome, take root, and see the environment as one they fully inhabit and not just one that is tolerant of them (Rendon, 2021)? We desperately need to diversify our leadership structure as many organizations currently do, both to protect the progress we have made and to help us proactively prepare for what is coming next. This will also hopefully protect those who are doing the DEI heavy lifting because there will be more than one of each diverse person strategically planning our next steps, but also to make sure those that are still in observer roles see genuine and sustained commitment to advancing DEI (Bui, 2019; Rendon, 2021). We also need that to ensure that the environment is one in which everyone feels able to vocalize what they need and would like to see change (Rendon, 2021). The reward for completing all of these activities was still more work. We are in the early stages of a retention initiative for our diverse and minoritized community members. That will likely take another year to plan, implement, and assess. However, resting on our laurels is not possible when there really are a limited number of us available to push the agenda forward.

HOW CAN YOU HELP THE BLACK WOMEN IN YOUR MIDST?

I have already mentioned properly empowering them to do their work, but I will say it again. We don't want people to fear the work that these women are doing, but we do need people to take things seriously. We also want people to seek out the DEI experts so that they don't tackle projects badly. I can share this because it is a clear example of what I am referring to about bad execution. I was approached by a department after they had received some negative feedback on a piece of advertisement. I was asked to review the feedback and the ad to see what could have prompted the reaction they received. It was pretty clear what the problem was with the original ad. It resulted from people not fully understanding the language they were using and how it might read to diverse populations. I wish they had touched based ahead of the original ad, but to their credit they rewrote the ad, apologized for the mistake, and asked that others reach out with thoughts or concerns if they had any. I was able to diffuse the situation and build a new relationship that has proven to be successful.

You need to pay these women for the work that they are doing. This is extra labor. This is often emotionally taxing labor where Black women have to balance their job roles versus their personal experiences and expertise. This is also often unappreciated work with those in DEI roles receiving pushback from their colleagues. So yes, pay them for the work they are doing, that they encourage you to do, and that typically comes with increased mentoring and other support requests. As you are paying them, make sure that you are not creating income inequities between them and non-Black employees who may be in the same roles within your company or external to it (Bui, 2019). Sometimes that work is devalued because the person doing it is a Black woman and that is also problematic. If you value the work, then value the person doing the work period and compensate them fairly.

Make sure that those women are okay. This does not mean the obligatory hey how are you conversation we routinely have at the beginning of a meeting or that we share in passing. This is a literal check in meeting with those women on a regular basis. It's necessary for those who are doing the DEI work but would be helpful for everyone. While the work environment became stressful for a different reason, one of my former employers asked me very directedly where I needed to go or what I had to do if I wanted to bask in Blackness to recharge myself. He didn't ask because he wanted to participate himself. He was an older and very white cisgender man. He asked because he knew our area was tough to live in if you were not white. I could routinely count ten or more confederate flags on vehicles or flag poles as I drive the fifteen minutes from my place of employment to my home in a neighboring city. The flag bearers would tell me it wasn't a sign of hate as they simultaneously complained about Black students on campus and Black athletes not playing well. I don't think my boss would have considered himself a diversity advocate, especially not in the early part of this century, but he checked in on me more often than he had to because he wanted me to feel at home in my space and with my colleagues. I appreciated that and often share his words of wisdom with others. Definitely check on Black women after major DEI goals are achieved. While I had colleagues who I could debrief with, it would have also been nice if my leadership team had said "hey, how are you feeling?" I'm decidedly proud of what we have done thus far but some of those wins came with heightened stress and trepidation. I was not sure the training requirement would pass based on our dialogue. That made me unsure of how I would continue to work collaboratively with people who couldn't see the benefit of a very brief, self-selected training that should ultimately help them do their jobs more effectively. I did not have to sort that out but I did have to admit to myself that I had been keyed up and ultimately afraid that we had done all of this work for nothing.

Ask them about the unpaid mentoring or labor that they are currently participating in for the betterment of your organization. I have always had quite a few people approach me every semester to pick my brain on things. This could be students looking to go to graduate school or colleagues thinking about how to craft a job ad to attract the most diverse field. I am happy to support them because again this ends up helping all of us in the long run. However, that work, when finally documented, amounts to three to four extra hours a week during busier periods but at least an hour every week. It translated to twenty-five-plus students who were admitted to a variety of graduate programs, more than one hundred students taken to conferences to present or network, lengthy conversations with colleagues about mistakes they may have made, want to avoid, or have seen others commit while also reminding them the easiest thing to do is to model the behavior they want to see and apologize when they slip up. It all adds up and it all requires investment in self-care or encouragement from leadership to protect those women. Once you have a fuller picture of all the work they do for your organization, make sure as much of that as possible is compensated then make sure they have the support they need to keep doing it well.

Equally as important to the other suggestions is for the leadership to maintain its public and pronounced commitment to diversity. Do not let it be part of a strategic plan and never executed or repeated in following planning cycles. Do not let a change in leadership allow the work to slip off the radar. If you do, the original problem will never be fully resolved, and a series of exhausting initiatives will come and go without the buy in that is needed to sustain change. Even if the strategy changes, make sure that your leadership team, your organization, and your DEI employees have a thru line to carry forward into each new project and planning period. Give yourself the space and time to assess what worked and give the Black women doing the work time to process how to proceed with your goals in mind. Listen to them intently and make sure their expertise is allowed to inform your decision making while you acquire your own.

CONCLUSION

I go to a lot of trainings because I am seen as an expert in this realm. I appreciate that I am selected and try to learn something from each session to bring back to my organization. What resonated with me most recently in addition to everything that I have covered is that we have to make this process more about collaborative growth than just increasing the number of Black women or DEI professionals in decision-making roles. To be clear, we definitely need more people doing the work and we need to have more Black women in leadership roles (Bui, 2019; Rendon, 2021). However, if we just leave the responsibility of making groups, organizations, or people better then we are collectively passing the buck to a few people and will not assume responsibility for goals not being met. Yes, trust your experts but also assess where you have blind spots and what are you going to do to address them.

If you wonder why you cannot find Black or Latina or Asian women to hire in certain middle leadership roles, you do not look at your current system to see what you are doing to get those women ready for those positions then you have a blind spot. I enjoy my work in the classroom and believe that my students need to see me more than I need to be a chair or a dean right now. However, there is also usually no clear path out of the classroom if you are not mentored to assume that role in the future. If as a hiring manager, you cannot figure out why your job pools are always homogenous then you have a blind spot. Where are you advertising? Who are you reaching out to when you have a new opening? How diverse is your personal network if you asked them to share your job ad? If you are looking at your classroom and see a lack of students that reflect the populations they will serve and you don't think there's more you could actively do to recruit, then you have a blind spot. Is it your area that does not afford you a more diverse student population or is it how you are presenting the profession? Or worse yet, is it because the teaching staff doesn't reflect the population they want to serve as well?

In those cases, ask questions and go to trainings and then ask more questions and go to more trainings. There is no arrival point when it comes to DEI work. There is always more to do as long as the system operates as it does.

We have to be prepared to handle what is present, know that it was informed by things that happened in the past, and plan for ways to mitigate inequities in the future. That's true no matter what our field is and what our plans should reflect. We have to be flexible and understand that we won't always get it right. When we stumble, as the department did earlier, we should apologize and acknowledge that we did not perform at the level we aspire to perform. Collectively though, we need to understand that this is a group effort. While someone may be the group leader, we each have to learn what we can to play our roles most effectively. If we can do that, we make it easier for Black women and other women of color to grow and thrive in our spaces and as was stated in a previous chapter—everyone succeeds when Black women succeed (Bofino et al., 2021). So let's all win.

REFERENCES

Apugo, D. (2019). A hidden culture of coping: Insights on African American Women's existence in predominately white spaces. *Multicultural Perspectives, 21*(1), 53–62.

Bertrand, M., and Mullainathan, S. (2003). Are Emily and Greg more employable than Lakisha and Jamal? A field experiment on labor market discrimination. *National Bureau of Economic Research*, Working Paper 9873.

Bofino, B. A., Zafar, R., Maguire, J., and Mintz, M. (June 8, 2021). "How the advancement gf Black Women will build a better economy for all." www.spglobal.com/en/research-insights/featured/how-the-advancement-of-black-women-will-build-a-better-economy-for-all.

Bui, O. (2019). Race to lead: Women of color in the nonprofit sector. *Building Movement Project.*

Culver, J. D. (2018). *Pursuing the professoriate: The academic career development of Black female doctoral students at predominantly White institutions* (Publication No. 10928772) [Doctoral dissertation University of Missouri St. Louis]. ProQuest Dissertations & Theses Global.

Du Bois, W. E. B. (1903). *The Souls of Black Folks*. A. C. McClurg & Sons.

Jackson, W. (June 1, 2022). "Steve Wilks Comments on Why He Joined Brian Flores's Lawsuit." *Sports Illustrated.*

Kline, P., Rose, E. K., and Walters, C. R. (2021). Systemic discrimination among large U.S. employers. *National Bureau of Economic Research*, Working Paper 29053. www.nber.org/papers/w29053.

Miller, J. (October 12, 2020). "Their bosses asked them to lead diversity reviews. Guess why." *New York Times.*

Rendon, J. (January 1, 2021). The challenges of being a woman leader of color. *Chronicle of Philanthropy, 33*(3), 14.

Spencer, B. M., Artis, S., Shavers, M., LeSure, S., and Joshi, A. (2022). To code-Switch or not to code-switch: The psychosocial ramifications of being resilient Black women engineering and computing doctoral students. *Sociological Focus, 55*(2), 130–150, DOI: 10.1080/00380237.2022.2054482.

Chapter 9

Random Reflections at 3 A.M.

Sharon L. Bowman

"You don't act like one of those university people. You act like a real person." I quickly learned this was one of the highest compliments one could receive from the local community, especially from the Black community, in my new home in Indiana. In Muncie, you are not "from here" unless you were "born here," no matter how long you live here. If I raised children in this community, they could be from here, but I never would. And being connected to the university made it even less likely I could be accepted, as this is a true town-and-gown community if there ever was one. I volunteered my time for the local Planned Parenthood chapter in my early years in town, as they worked to open an office that would be welcoming to the local Black community. I was one of a few university employees on the planning board, but probably the *only* one (Black or White) who heard that line. So, as I said, I understood the statement above as the compliment it was meant to be, and accepted it, of course; but still, here was yet another time and place in which I didn't quite fit into either the Town or the Gown world.

It was 1989; I was also a twenty-eight-year-old new psychology faculty member on a campus with maybe ten to fourteen African American faculty. I was the only one in my department, replacing the Black man who left Indiana mid-year for Michigan. Fun fact: his wife, also a PhD in psychology, worked at the university's counseling center. I cannot recall the number of people who assumed I *must* be replacing her, and not him. As it turned out, there was one other Black faculty member in my college; he was the first Black faculty member ever hired at the university, and the first to be tenured and promoted. At the beginning of each year, he and I would stand at the back of the college's opening faculty meeting and note the number of Black faces. For the record, most of the time in the early years we were the only ones. As you can imagine, my jeans and t-shirt, or pointedly otherwise casually dressed,

Black body stood out in a crowd of White faculty dressed in stereotypical sport coats and proper skirts. My then-dean, an older White man, scowled at me without comment weekly if we caught the elevator together. The majority of my students, I teach in a primarily graduate department, were my age or older. Like I said, I didn't quite fit in to either the Town or Gown world back then. I probably fit in better now, but sometimes I still stand outside and wonder how I got here.

As is true of most of the other authors in this book, I am many things to many people. Professionally, I am a counseling psychologist; my training is reflected in every single thing I do. I have been a college professor for more than half my life, working at the first position I took after graduation (no, I never thought I'd be here this long). I have been chair of my department for most of that time. I was the first Black chair at the university, in fact. I also have a small clinical practice on the side. In the profession, I have served on more than my share of leadership boards for multiple organizations, including being president or chair of at least three of them. I even ran for president of the largest psychological association in the world. I came in third of five, and have no shame in saying that the two psychologists, both BIPOC, who bested me definitely earned the right to have that position. Before you assume that my intent is to brag, anyone who knows me will assure you that I don't brag. I share the depth of my background because it is *fact*, and women are socialized to not draw attention to ourselves for our efforts and successes (Fielding-Singh et al., 2018; Fox & Ferri, 1992). We "should" remain humble, and focus on the collective, and wait until someone else notices us. The problem with that approach is that men aren't waiting around to be noticed. They will tell the world what they did and expect accolades, even if their boasting fails to acknowledge the woman standing beside them who actually did the work (and in many cases, more work than her counterpart). While this level of undervaluing happens for all women, as Black women, we must change the narrative for ourselves.

I have had the privilege of reading/editing all the other chapters in this book before writing my own. Their stories, triumphs, injuries, and visions for the future stirred so many stories from my own history that I periodically had to just step away and stop reading for a moment to regroup. However, doing the review also allowed the puzzle pieces of my own chapter to take shape in the recesses of my mind. Multitasking is a thing, right? As a result, I have decided to highlight some of the steps that have shaped my career. It helps to be on the far side of the rainbow, and able to see much of my journey in retrospect.

BE A LEADER, NOT A FOLLOWER

I am, at my core, the eldest child and only daughter of my parents, Ralph and Helen Bowman. I often state that I am a reflection of both of them. My Georgia-born mother was an introvert; she would sit with the neighbor women and listen to them gossip about husbands, kids, and jobs, but my mother rarely had a thing to add. She could keep a secret. She was not the one to be in the middle of someone else's drama, but she probably knew all about it. From her, I learned to sit and listen, to watch the process play out, and to figure out the rules of engagement before stepping into the mix of things. Verbally, I can be invisible if I choose to be. As one of the few, or usually the only, Black faces in the crowd, I clearly didn't disappear entirely, but I don't offer an opinion until I am sure. As you might imagine, my mother's reticence has done me well in my chosen field.

My Ohio-born father, on the other hand, was the middle child of five. He never hesitated to share his opinion on any topic and cared little whether anyone wanted to hear it. As far back as I can remember, he did not know a stranger; he could strike up a conversation with any passing individual. There was always something to learn, something to talk about. My father was a mail carrier throughout my life, until the summer I graduated with my doctoral degree; thus, he has ample opportunity to talk to a wide variety of people. To be sure, he did not back down from a challenge, no matter the age or ethnicity of the other person. He was always very clear with me about two things: first, I should always be the leader, not a follower. If you are the leader, you have no one to blame but yourself if you get into trouble, but you also have a much better chance of making the situation work to your advantage. Second, do not wait for someone else who "looks like you" (rubbing his finger along his arm here) to do something that you want to do. Waiting for someone else to come along first could result in never getting to do whatever it is. If you want to participate in an activity, *go do it*; you have every right to do it. I don't suffer fools gladly, especially when it comes to disordered leadership. As a result, my father sits on my shoulder each time I step into a leadership role because I don't like the way things are being handled (and I know I can do it at least as well as the incumbents). He is also with me when I plow into an activity (social or professional) and there is no one else in the space who "looks like me." I can't be bothered about that; I just need to make sure I stay safe and sane.

In short, my parents taught me how to be a Black woman in a world that doesn't necessarily know what to do with us. Though they themselves did not finish college, they agreed with my sixth-grade teacher (a white man) that I was college material. They supported me all along the way, understanding enough to know that my academic world was different from my upbringing. They didn't always agree with my choices (honestly, there were choices made that I never told them about because I knew it would mean trouble), but always, always expected me to put school first. Their support, guidance, and sense of direction shaped my understanding of myself as a Black woman, and my goal of mentoring those who follow me.

I will try to end each section with a suggestion, either for you or for someone else. This suggestion is obvious: do not let someone else define you or tell you who or what you have to be, based on their standard. I watched and learned the rules, then made my own decisions about whether and how to break them. If I waited until I saw someone else do "it," whatever it was, I would never have lived the life I've had. I have been the first, or the only, Black woman in sight for a lot of the things I have done in my life. However, curiosity and a sense of adventure outweighed the fear almost every time. I learned something, even from the less successful experiences.

IMPOSTER PHENOMENON PERSONIFIED

Several other authors mentioned the concept of imposter phenomenon. Clance and Imes (1978) first defined it as the internal sense or belief that we are not as competent as others perceive us to be; we are just waiting for someone to call us out for not belonging where we are. They were originally referencing high-achieving women, but I see it across the board in my students, my junior colleagues, and—even now—sometimes in myself. It is not unusual to feel like a fraud, especially in new situations like taking on a new job or starting school in a new community (Maftei et al., 2021; Fox & Ferri, 1992). Each year, I watch my new cohort of doctoral students jockey for position, and it is clear most of them are convinced they don't really belong with their smarter, more talented, more competent, more experienced colleagues. I eventually comment that they are just waiting for me to walk in and say: "We made a mistake and admitted one of you erroneously. You know who you are; I will turn my back and you can just leave quietly." The problem is, left to their own devices half the class would actually leave.

Women of color are particularly susceptible to imposter phenomenon. Why? It seems that all the usual environmental problems with racism, classism, sexism, and stereotyping, along with the lack of similar role models, come into play. We operate in systems in which the male (usually, but not only, White) standard is our comparison group. We cannot completely fit that standard, no matter how we try. Sometimes, frankly, we just give up. I noted earlier that I started this position as a child, being nearly ten years younger than the next closest faculty member. I was one of three women; the other two had children my age. The observer in me (thanks, mom!) watched the dynamics in faculty meetings for weeks. I learned that there were two sets of rules: white men (the majority) could speak at will, but some White men could speak over other White men. White women, no matter how seasoned and respected, no matter how feminist-posturing, could always, always be spoken over by any man in the room. After a while, I realized that I was not a White man, nor am I a White woman, so those rules would not work for me. Once I decided to actually speak in a meeting, I had to shut down men who tried to speak over me (yes, I got a version of the Angry Black Woman moniker, but I also shut that down). I worked past my more innate reticence and spoke out when it was important, making it clear that I didn't care how, or if, they decided to respond to my comments, but I would be finishing those comments in their entirety before someone took the floor from me. To this day, it is rare for someone to interrupt me.

I share this story with you, as I do with my students, as a reminder that our voices deserve to be heard as much as anyone's does. No one can speak for us, and we can strive to change the rules. I loved reading Tulshyan and Burey's (2021) article, as they have given me a new perspective. Imposter phenomenon focuses on the individual as though she is the problem, but instead perhaps we should stop blaming the victim and look to shifting the system? What would it mean to help other Black women (or, really, any woman of color) re-center the crux of the issue from the individual to the system? Maybe, just maybe, we wouldn't all be so tired, we wouldn't all be trying to catch up or keep up with, to get ahead of, the perceived leaders.

My suggestion to combat imposter phenomenon, then, is twofold. If you feel the pain welling up in yourself, *stop*, *look*, and *listen*. *Stop* your cycle of self-flagellation for not doing enough, for not belonging, for not being enough. You are more than enough; you might even be "extra," but too bad. *Look* at your vita, your webpage, your awards, your genuine thank-you notes from students and colleagues. You did that work, and with a moment's thought you will remember the pain you went through to get it all done. You earned those accolades, sister; no one wrote that paper for you. And if the first two steps don't snap you out of the cycle, then *listen* as your trusted peers and mentors set you free. You are not too busy, or isolated, or ashamed to take the time to reach out for some much-needed re-centering. Many of us are willing (or expected) to do this for others, but cannot figure out how to reach out for ourselves. I am just going to say this out loud: not reaching out is very likely one of the reasons for our high suicide rate; we have got to take care of our mental health (Walker, 2020).

Second, if you suspect someone else is questioning her self-worth, her sense of belongingness, throw her a lifeline. I have a tendency to toss compliments out of the blue, just because I have been thinking about someone, or because I've heard second- or third-hand about some miraculous work someone has done and I need them to know about it. Send an email, a text, or buy a stamp and send an actual snail mail note (yes, I believe in the power of a handwritten note that I can hold, cherish, and return to when I need a boost). If you think she needs to see your face, to have a good cry and scream, or both, then make time for her to do that. We are not good at asking for what we need, which is why *you* may have to reach out to *her* to pull her off the ledge.

PUT SOME RESPEC' ON MY NAME

Early in my teaching career, one of my male doctoral students consistently called me by my first name, but my White male colleagues were all "Dr. So-and-So." Mind you, said student and I were the same age, and my colleagues were all older. One day I informed the student that henceforth I would be on par with the others—either we were all Dr. or we were all casual. He argued with me that I was just being petty because I had a new PhD. I had to remind him that freshness stamp on my degree was not the issue; the respect and misogyny was. Further, as an ethnic minority man himself, he would find out differently once *he* graduated. This was a battle to be fought with others over the years. Truth be told, I don't usually have a need to pull out the title, even in many professional situations, unless someone is being disrespectful and starting on the wrong foot. Most recently, a Black male undergraduate student got crossways with one of his instructors and wanted to file a complaint. I emailed him to ask the nature of his complaint; he responded with something to the effect of "Hi, Sharon." Uh, no. Just no. I had already noticed he referred to his doctoral student instructor and her faculty supervisor, both women, by their first names, so I could see this coming. My response: "My name is not Sharon; it is Dr. Bowman. Now, what can I do for you?" He chose to not respond to me at that moment; long story but let me add that he later angrily told me I was automatically supposed to be on his side because I am a Black woman. Again, no; that is not how it works in my world. I worked a little too hard to earn my creds and will not throw them away just because you have some melanin (and that was true even before I read the book on him).

There are plenty of links on Reddit, Yahoo, and other sites asking whether it is okay to call a professor by his/her/their first name. Clearly, undergraduates are confused by this; well, okay, graduates are, too. However, the literature on the dynamics of calling male vs. female professors by their first names is enlightening. Professors are perceived with more respect when called by their titles; female professors using the title were also perceived as less accessible (Takiff et al., 2001). Male professors are more likely than female professors to be called by their title over their first name. Thus, female professors can be accessible or hold status in the eyes of students, but not both. This is not a choice any of us should have to make. Oddly, a 2020 study of the implications of clarifying one's preferred title in an email did not assess differences by sex; in fact, they purposely used a gender-neutral prompt (despite citing the Takiff et al., 2001, article).

This issue of what title to use makes me tired for several reasons. First, although I say that personally I don't stress about it, I realized in writing this that I do, in fact, get upset when someone mistitles me who should be more respectful. I know it is a sign of privilege, but if I don't pull out the title, I can easily be mistaken for support staff, or a parent, or even a student—and sadly be overlooked and dismissed. A Black male athlete came to my office to lodge a complaint after being admonished by his coach about his attitude. I happened to be sitting at the reception desk when he arrived, haughtily demanding to speak to Miss Bowman (yep, he did). Imagine his surprise when he learned that Dr. Bowman was a Black woman; attitude changed immediately. Second, I also hold power by virtue of being department chair. My junior faculty, however, do not hold that power role. Further, they look like our students, and have the same issues I had as new faculty with gaining respect. I share with them that they have the right to decide their title, and to insist on Dr. if that is what they prefer. It is not a pretension; they gave blood for that degree. For the record, I have noted that it is generally White men in my department advocating for the "first names for everyone" approach across the board; that push has never come from a woman or person of color in my experience.

My suggestion here is: define for yourself who you are, then own your identity without shame or challenge. You worked for that degree, that license, that certification; no one can take it from you or shame you for choosing to use it. All the pain of earning the doctorate was worth it when "Dr. Bowman" had to go forward and contact a physician's office to challenge apparent mistreatment of one of our mutual clients/patients. I remind my students that "Dr. Bowman" can sometimes break through a barrier a client is facing faster than the client can, or can get feedback from the licensure board. Use your power for the good, and teach your trainees to do the same; they cannot change the world unless they step up.

YEAH, BUT DO YOU KNOW WHERE THEY ARE?

Several of our co-authors have mentioned the weight that being a mentor or role model carries. There are days, and nights, in which I don't think I can carry one more child across the finish line. Fortunately, those days are balanced with getting to hug one more "baby" at graduation or getting to cheer when someone drops by to share that they have landed a job, or gotten licensed, or been admitted to a doctoral program. While I have never birthed a biological child, I have more children out in the world than any Black woman should have.

I have been both mentor and role model over my three decades of practice. There is a distinction between the two (Gotian, 2021). A role model is someone you look up to, someone you want to emulate. There is every possibility you have never met this person, and never will, and even more likely that person has no idea that you consider him/her/them a role model. A mentor, on the other hand, is a living, breathing person who is your guide, your cheerleader, and sometimes your conscience, as you travel along the path. I'm not talking about officially assigned mentors here, that is, when your academic program or your workplace pairs you with a "mentor." I refer here to a mutually agreed-upon, chosen relationship between you and the other person (those officially sanctioned relationships may also be a chosen one, of course). There is an abundant literature discussing the effects of mentoring on Black women in higher education (c.f. Crawford & Smith, 2005; Patton & Harper, 2003; Rasheem et al., 2018). And, if you are interested in a formal mentoring program, again, there are plenty of examples to be found in quick search of the internet.

My personal experience as a mentee harkens back to graduate school and the early years of employment. My doctoral advisor was a White man, well renowned in the field. He taught me what I needed to know about being a faculty member and made sure I had the graduate school experiences to set me up for success. I will be forever in his debt for that, and for his insistence that I should become a professor (I was not interested and was vocal in my dissent). He also introduced me to a role model, one of the pioneering Black women in my field. She happened to call him one day while I was in his office, and he handed me the phone. She informed me, this Black child she had never laid eyes on, that if my advisor said I should join the academy I should do exactly that. *Period.* I was not a stupid child; I understood that this voice from Boston was to be heeded. So, while I did not publicly embrace my decision until two years later, that was the day I knew I was to follow in her footsteps. A couple of years after I graduated, she and I, along with another fresh Black female faculty member, were at a conference. I reminded her of that call; she didn't recall it, but she believed it could have happened that way. The three of us began counting the number of Black women faculty in our field we could identify; I think the number was around fourteen. Trust me when I say that I am here, in this field, because my advisor pushed me, and my role model set the pace.

On the other side of the desk, though, once you accept the title it is difficult to *not* keep doing what you do. I acknowledge that I chose to become a professor at a predominantly White institution (PWI) because I saw almost no one who "looks like me" in this role throughout my education. I knew that Black students at Black institutions would have plenty of representation, but those at PWIs would not. I also knew that I could not complain about the lack of representation if I was not willing to throw myself into the mix for hiring. I was prepared for the hiring process and prepared for the teaching part of the process. What I was *not* prepared for were the demands on my time for every Black undergraduate organization in need of a speaker, or Student Affairs office in need of a Black professional to show up, or Academic Affairs demands to serve on X, Y, or Z committee. I eventually began to ask, directly, whether I was approached to serve the "token" spot on the committee; then I could decide accordingly whether I was interested in accepting the request. I remembered the advice I had been given by someone older and wiser than me: do not accept all of these requests, especially if they do not count toward promotion and tenure. You cannot be an influence if you are unable to get tenured because you didn't meet the basic requirements of the position; in short, put on your own oxygen mask before helping someone else with theirs.

The harder part of mentoring, or just supporting, students is recognizing how many people are seeking support. In my early years, it seemed like every graduate student who was not a cis-gender White man was at my door. We had a critical mass of Black students, most of whom were attached to me at the hip (again—only person who looked like them in sight). I could deal with that; I could deal with them making my house their gathering spot because it felt safe, or dropping by my office just to check in. What I was not prepared for were my White colleagues, who subtly, or in one case openly, suggested that I was "hoarding" the minority students from them. If Professor X was looking for a student, it was not uncommon to come by my office and ask me where said student was, or to knock on my door and assume the student was in my office already. I blew up one day and explained that I have better things to do than hoard all of the diverse students. If my colleagues wanted the students' attention, then they should proactively reach out to the students themselves instead of accusing me of gatekeeping. That put a stop to most of this drama. Of course, it didn't keep me from being tired; I look back at those days and I do not know how I survived to tenure.

These days, I continue to support as many students and junior professionals as I can, but I am working on re-centering myself. It is still true that I cannot be supportive if I am not taking care of myself, so I am trying to be better about my own time and health. I try to be there for my direct advisees, but because they worry about bothering me they are sometimes hesitant to ask for my time. I make it clear that I absolutely will show up if they tell me they need me, and sometimes I magically show up even if they have only conjured me up in the minds (hence my reputation for sending emails at 3 A.M.). However, my advisees are forewarned to be careful what they wish for; the full measure of my attention can be very hard to handle. Most people prefer getting glancing blows instead of head-on views. As one student said recently, I don't always tell them what they want to hear, but I will tell them what they need to hear.

My suggestion for mentoring is simple: be your genuine self. If you are seeking a mentor, step up and ask for what you need. Please do not assume that we automatically know; not every Black woman I meet wants, or needs, to be mentored by me. If I don't know what you are looking for, I may not give you what you are seeking, and we may both end up disappointed. Also remember that seeking mentorship does not mean you should only have one at a time. I had several mentors at the same time, because they fulfilled different needs on a personal and/or professional level. My White male advisor taught me to be a professor and to operate within our professional associations, but he could not tell me about being a Black woman PhD. I needed someone else to do that. Seek what you need from a variety of trustworthy sources and accept that the roles and needs will change over time. In any case, listen to the gifts you receive, weigh their value carefully, and determine how well they applies to your situation. Then use the gifts accordingly. If you are asked to be, or offering to be, a mentor, take the role seriously. Share with your mentee both the positive and the constructive aspects of what you do, what you see, and what you want from them. Do as much listening as you do talking; sometimes my mentee simply needs me to be a sounding board. Guidance may just mean making suggestions, or laying out options, and encouraging the mentee to move down her path. It may mean hearing her out when she comes to you expressing cultural paranoia, or imposter syndrome, or righteous anger. And, eventually, it will mean letting the relationship evolve to a new stage, possibly even a more equal footing. I promise you, that stage almost always makes the previous stress worthwhile.

MY SUPER-SECRET, NOT-SO-SECRET PLAN

If you made it this far, you have some idea of the inner working of my brain. There is another reason that I teach, that I do all the things that I do. I want to help shape the next generation, to train those who come behind me to go on to change their little bit of the world. When I feel undervalued, I can look at the thirty-odd students whose dissertations I have chaired over the years; half of those students have been BIPOC, queer, and/or religious minorities. I see the future in what they do, and it bolsters my energies a bit. When I feel overwhelmed, which is a feeling that waxes and wanes in my professional world, I also see my replacements coming. I see in them what my advisor, and my role model, saw in me so many years ago: the potential to carry the message forward.

REFERENCES

Clance, P. R., & Imes, S. A. (1978). The imposter phenomenon in high achieving women: Dynamics and therapeutic intervention. *Psychotherapy: Theory, Research & Practice, 15*(3), 241–247.doi.org/10.1037/h0086006.

Crawford, K., & Smith, D. (2005). The We and the Us: Mentoring African American Women. *Journal of Black Studies, 36*(1), 52–67. http://www.jstor.org/stable/40027321.

Fox, M. F., & Ferri, V. C. (1992). Women, men, and their attributions for success in academe. *Social Psychology Quarterly, 55*(3), 257–271.

Fielding-Singh, P., Magliozzi, D., & Ballakrishnen, S. (August 28, 2018). "Why women stay out of the spotlight at work." *Harvard Business Review.* hbr.org/2018/08/why-women-stay-out-of-the-spotlight-at-work.

Gotian, R. (January 24, 2021). Role model, mentor, coach, or sponsor: Which do you need? *Psychology Today.* www.psychologytoday.com/us/blog/optimizing-success/202101/role-model-mentor-coach-or-sponsor-which-do-you-need.

Hildenbrand, G. M., Perrault, E. K., & Devine, T. M. (2020). You may call me Professor: Professor form of address in email communication and college student reactions to not knowing what to call their professors. *Journal of Communication Pedagogy, 3,* 82–99. DOI: 10.31446/JCP2020.08.

Maftei, A., Dumitriu, A., & Holman, A.-C. (2021). "They will discover I'm a fraud." The imposter syndrome among psychology students. *Studia Psychologica, 63*(4), 337–351.

Patton, L. D., & Harper, S. (2003). Mentoring relationships among African American women in graduate and professional schools. *New Directions for Student Services, 2003*(104), 67–78. DOI: 10.1002/ss.108.

Rasheem, S., Alleman, A-S., Mushonga, D., Anderson, D., & Ofahengaue Vakalahi, H. F. (2018). Mentor-shape: Exploring the mentoring relationships of Black women in doctoral programs. *Mentoring & Tutoring: Partnership in Learning.* DOI:10.1080/13611267.2018.1445443.

Takiff, H. A., Sanchez, D. T., & Stewart, T. (2001). What's in a name? The status implications of students' terms of address for male and female professors. *Psychology of Women Quarterly, 25*(2), 134–144.

Tulshyan, R., & Burey, J-A. (February 11, 2021). Stop telling women they have Imposter Syndrome. *Harvard Business Review.* Hbr.org/2021/02/stop-telling-women-they-have-imposter-syndrome.

Walker, R. (2020). *The Unapologetic Guide to Black Mental Health: Navigate an Unequal System, Learn Tools for Emotional Wellness, and Get the Help You Deserve*. Oakland, CA: New Harbinger Publications, Inc.

Conclusion

Overworked and Undervalued, a Culmination

Rosalyn D. Davis and Sharon L. Bowman

As we start to close out this volume, let us just say that we may not be as articulate as we hoped at the beginning of this exercise. It was an intense labor to birth the last nine personal chapters you have read. At different points in the writing process, we all struggled to get words on paper. Not because we didn't possess the words, but because reliving the moments we shared, we few exceptions, brought up emotions we thought we had fully processed but found out mid-sentence were still sensitive. That's a strange feeling for the collective of women involved in this manuscript, just so we're clear. The second author of this chapter had to check in with each author, as well as herself, to figure out what the stumbling block was to getting the words in our brains and mouths onto these very blank pages. Even with that, and acknowledging that we had a lot to share, it took last gasping breaths of writing to arrive here now. After lots of conversation and internal pondering about what was causing the collective writing block, two things came to the forefront.

The first was that, much like the title of this text, we were all in varying degrees of overwork and feeling undervalued. Since we moved forward with this project, everyone has been employed full time in at least one job, but often our full-time work involved extra projects, classes, presentations, or demands. All of us were still being called on to be leaders in research, mentoring, diversity work, or some combination of all three. And all of us were still needing to take care of ourselves, our families, our communities, and our friends. There was not a summer off to write or an uninterrupted break to focus. These words had to hit paper in between everything else that had to be done. We gathered together partly because of our shared understanding of being asked to be and do the things we do so ultimately the lack of time is not entirely surprising. The second issue was much more surprising for all of us. There was a trauma involved with releasing these stories. No matter how much we have progressed from the incidents or stores we shared with you, there are still portions of the story that sit with us and make it difficult to carry forward with it in our daily consciousness. Once we processed that aspect of the writing block, it became easier to slowly share out what is on these pages.

You have received honest and personal snapshots into the lives of Black women who are blessed with enough education to not be treated as poorly as we otherwise might be. Those of us with doctorates may be met with surprise but we also receive a level of respect that is not available to the Black female grocery store clerk. Those of us working in professional positions have the benefit of steady income and health care. That allows us to try to medically treat the long-term impact of stress and racism that impact us disproportionately as we move throughout the world. You also saw an immense amount of collaboration throughout these chapters. As we continued our work, working together gave us the ability and opportunity to combine energy and share the emotional load. Those chapters blossomed in ways they likely would not have otherwise, and we are grateful to each other that we willingly set aside ego to achieve our goal.

We are not sure who is ultimately going to peruse these pages. However, we hope that for those that do, that you have learned about what it means for each of us to be Black women in the United States at this particular moment in history. Our stories may have been presented differently had this come to your attention a year ago, or prior to the pandemic. We were different and the world we existed in was different. What you have now is more transparent, even as we do not fully disclose every bad moment or problem we have ever encountered.

WHAT YOU HAVE SEEN FOR CERTAIN

You have seen us share a few common concepts. This wasn't intentional but they were shared points of connection as we wrote. If you haven't heard of or read works by W. E. B. Du Bois prior to this text, then we hope you are intrigued enough to do so now. His work shaped a lot of the early discourse around how formerly enslaved Blacks may be able to succeed in American society. *The Souls of Black Folks* is required reading at a lot of Historically Black Colleges and Universities (HBCUs), which is one reason why it was present in so many of our stories as HBCU graduates. However, there is not a better way to describe what it is like to be a minoritized person in American culture than double consciousness (Du Bois, 1903). We grow up needing to understand how American culture, and thus whiteness, operates. This is for both our protection and our potential success. Double consciousness can encompass everything from how we speak, dress, what we name our children, where we live, the groups we join, and ultimately, how much of our own culture we embrace. We also must understand that while we are impacted by systems of whiteness that we are ourselves are not White. Understanding what it means to be a young Black woman in areas where we may be the only one in our immediate circles because our parents wanted to give us a chance to succeed and moved us to better school districts or safer areas. That success may also come with a disconnect from Black culture that has a tenuous relationship with the American education system. We do not willingly abandon who we are but may be seen as outsiders by those who do not join us on that particular journey. So there is an inherent struggle in being one of the hyphenated Americans. Even when we have lived here for hundreds of years, portions of the culture will always "other" us despite what we may have done to assimilate into the dominant culture. It also begs the question: why do we have to assimilate to be seen as fully American?

You have also seen us discuss various struggles with whiteness not making room for our Blackness. Being told you are unprofessional or impolite because you are laughing loudly and enjoying your day is so common an experience that Black women often have to decide where we will gather. Our laughs are rich and wonderful and we should not have to put them in check when we get a rare moment to breathe together. Those chuckles are hard earned and may only be afforded to us upon occasion because in other environments we are too much for those around us and end up muting our natural reactions. Being told you aren't friendly because you aren't smiling enough is also entirely too common an experience. It's almost as if these spaces only accommodate us because someone wants a sassy Black friend. We cannot be constant sources of entertainment. It doesn't allow us to be fully ourselves because we have been restricted to one facet of our personality. Having to carve out space for ourselves in environments not designed for us, we know how to do that. Not bringing ourselves to those spaces in the first place, now that is not something most of us are willing to do any longer, so please reread these chapters and prepare to make room for the big, talented personalities with big, gorgeous hair—that should not be touched without permission!—who are ready to make your acquaintances. This critique is not of White individuals, but of a system that has a very narrow view of what it means to be Black, woman, successful, intelligent, privileged, and so many other things. That system hurts everyone, including those who benefit from it as members of the dominant culture. That view is damaging because it implies that everyone can obtain it and ignores that lack of access most of us, regardless of what our complexion is, have to the resources we need to achieve that narrow piece of the pie.

You have also seen several of us struggle to meet our self-imposed responsibilities to our friends, family, and community while also maintaining a level of performance at work that can often marvel our colleagues. We aren't working more or harder because it seems like the best idea, but often because we wind up with a variety of job tasks that are uncompensated and somehow still crucial to the organization's success. We may have some expectations to mentor a student or a colleague from time to time. However, for Black women that often means being the go-to person for any or all BIPOC students and colleagues because there are rarely enough of us to each have a personal mentor. That mentoring often does not end when a student graduates or a colleague leaves their position. Most chapter authors may have had less to write about if we cut off our mentees when we made sure their degrees were in hand. Collectively, our fields are so small that once we find one another then we rarely lose contact as we move along our career paths because there is potentially no one else to ask.

Finally, you saw hurt and disappointment return to moments of clarity, hope, and joy. Things are by no means close to perfect for Black women right now, but we can start changing the narrative experience of the generations that come after us if stories like ours are read widely accepted and acted upon for the greater good. "The struggles make you stronger" is a bit trite but through this work, we were able to move beyond some of our stumbling blocks and release a collective sigh of relief. This process was cathartic, and we appreciate those who have been patient with us to get this work completed.

WHAT YOU DIDN'T SEE

As easy as it would have been to let loose and attack each person and incident where we felt personally wronged, we didn't engage in that exercise. We are tired, not bitter. We needed space to explain the difference between those mood states. It is exhausting to deal with these issues, yes, but anger punishes only us. To paraphrase an internet meme attributed to Tupac Shakur, "Just because we disagree doesn't mean I want you to starve. You just can't eat with me." Anger is easy. It demands no accountability, nor does it ask for any changes to be made; thus understanding can never be achieved. Plus, each and every one of us is tired of the Angry Black Woman trope. When Black women are angry, there's often a justifiable reason for that anger. Not letting us explore our full personalities is frustrating, as we have already discussed so we won't dig in our heels here.

You also didn't see us attack larger policy because there are so many different competing problems with current policy that it could become a separate book of its own. We kept everything very much at the level where each of us can be part of the solution to change things more immediately. If you are able to support the Black women in your sphere and impart larger changes, please do, but if all you can accomplish right now is making room for Black women to be great, then do that right now and we can tackle the larger things together later. Finally, you didn't see us try to account for every possible facet of Black womanhood. We shared our stories that we are sure lots of Black women can relate to, but we acknowledge the ways in which we are more privileged than some other groups of Black women.

WHAT WE HOPE YOU DO NEXT

As an individual your tasks are more pointed. First, we're going to be a little selfish and ask that you take some time and reread at least one chapter that deeply resonated with you because it might well describe a woman you personally know. Once you have done that, talk about that chapter with someone else, and if they seem intrigued, then share the book. Or better yet, encourage them to get their own copy of the book. Now that we are done promoting, what we really hope that you do is sit with what you have read and decide how much of an ally you have been to the Black women in your orbit. If you think you've been pretty good thus far, is there anything that you can do to get better? If you think you may have fallen short, take stock of what that is and try to make a targeted plan to do better.

As an organization, really do an analysis of how the Black women in your organization are doing. Are they part of your leadership team? If so, what roles do they represent? Are they gifted with fancy titles and no power, or do they get to impart genuine and sustainable change? If they are not present, why not? What is stopping you from facilitating change and promoting someone who is qualified to join your team? Are you prepared to do the heavy lifting of mentoring Black women so they can assume positions of leadership? If not, what steps do you need to take to start that process? Do you need to consult with other agencies that are doing that work already?

Your next steps require honest appraisal of where you are and where you would like to be. It also requires admitting when your structure won't support your goals and trying to assess how you can reform the environment to be positive and actively welcoming to all. It also requires patience but not stagnation. You will not achieve your goals overnight (do we ever achieve goals overnight?), but you cannot take so long to start making progress that people forget what they were working toward. Plan, execute, reassess, and restart the process if you need to do so. It may take a few failures before there is a resounding success but if you can stay the course you may ensure that the young Black women entering your organizations will flourish and help you achieve the next goals you can decide upon together. Because, ultimately, the diversity at the table helps the ideas abound and makes sure we don't leave anyone off the next agenda.

YOU HAVE OUR THANKS

We know that stories like ours are rarely told in public spaces, either because we aren't invited to share them or because we stumble on the words we want to share. There's a risk in being open for Black women that we each felt was worth revealing these narratives to a broader audience. While we have each other, there are other Black women struggling as the only person in their office, department, building, or street. The joy in hugging a woman who looks like us and understands us is indescribable. The fact that you are taking time to explore these stories with us is invaluable. We hope that we gave you some insight, some places to operate from to improve your environments, and some burgeoning interest in learning about those who could always benefit from a good ally or extended support system. Take care and be well.

REFERENCE

Du Bois, W. E. B. (1903). *The Souls of Black Folks.* A. C. McClurg & Sons.

Index

abilities, 6, 45–47, 49–50, 57, 63, 65, 89, 95, 97, 102, 105
ABW. *See* Angry Black Woman
academia, 24, 63, 67, 74–75, 77, 79
academic setting, 43, 70, 73, 75
advancement, 46, 63, 98, 106
advisor, 11–12, 45, 60–61, 69, 128, 131
African American, 1–16, 67, 81, 121, 131
African American students, 2–3, 10, 30
America, xii–xiii, 17, 34, 41, 55, 83–93
American culture, xii, 135
Americans, Black/African, 55, 76
Angry Black Woman (ABW), 8, 38–39, 55, 72, 125, 136

back-handed compliments, 7, 57
balance, work-life, 74, 76
belongingness, 2, 4–5, 125
benefits, ix, xii–xiii, xv, 14–15, 48, 50–51, 85, 87, 89, 91, 98, 134–35, 138
biases, 86–87, 101
BIPOC (Black, Indigenous, or other People of Color), 84, 89, 104, 122, 130
Black, 15, 19, 21–22, 31–33, 35, 55–59, 66–67, 70, 80, 84, 99–100, 118, 121; Indigenous, or other People of Color. *See* BIPOC
Black child, 56, 71, 102, 128
Black community, 95, 101, 103, 110, 121
Black culture, 19, 110, 135
Black Girl Magic, 1, 6–7, 11, 13, 95–107
Black people, 19, 32, 84, 98, 102–3
Black students, 18, 21, 57, 60, 129
Black woman, x, xii, 41, 44, 49, 95–96, 101–2, 112, 116, 123–24, 126–28, 130
Black women, ix–xvi, 12–13, 15, 23, 26–29, 31–34, 43–44, 47, 50, 95–106, 112–13, 116–19, 128, 134–38
blind spots, 25, 86, 118
bodies, 78, 95–97, 99–100
brilliance, 1–2, 13, 28

campus, 23–24, 28, 33, 43, 69, 81, 112, 114–15, 117, 121
care, 8, 23, 27, 33, 90–91, 97–98, 105–6, 109, 125, 129, 138
careers, 5–7, 12–13, 33, 43, 60, 64, 67, 74, 76–78, 98, 122
Caucasian students, 3, 10

change, 23–26, 74, 76, 80, 85–87, 91, 114–15, 117, 122, 125, 127, 130, 137
classroom, 3, 10, 32, 35, 52, 70, 74–75, 118
clients, 8–9, 23, 39, 75, 127
college, 3, 10, 43, 45, 47–48, 57–60, 65, 67, 90, 121
color, 2–3, 5–6, 8–10, 21–22, 64–65, 73–75, 86, 88–90, 92, 104–5, 109–19, 124–25, 127
communities, ix–x, 40, 43, 49, 85, 87–92, 98, 100–101, 104–5, 114, 133, 136; diverse, 87, 114–15; minoritized, 92, 115
complaint, 39, 126–27
connections, ix, 77, 87, 90, 96, 134
conversations, ix, xv, 33, 36, 38, 70, 74, 77, 86, 88–92, 110–12, 116–17, 123
counseling, 50, 85
counseling psychology, 17, 44, 85
courage, 51, 99–100
Covid-19, 29, 40, 77, 97, 106
co-workers, 5, 34–36, 38, 41, 95
culture, xiii, 5–6, 10–11, 19, 35, 86–87, 135

degrees, social work, 85
discrimination, 2–4, 8, 12, 15, 58, 63, 70–71; racial, 38–39
diversity, 3, 6–7, 14, 16, 21–22, 24–25, 67–68, 85, 88–89, 110, 117
dominant culture, 2, 4, 8, 12, 88, 135
Du Bois, 43, 53, 55, 80, 92–93, 102, 106, 112, 134–35, 138

economic research, 29, 119
education, 10, 12, 31–32, 50, 55–56, 61, 63–64, 81, 85, 87, 91, 93, 128–29
emotional support, 13, 64
emotional tax, xi, 6–7, 15
employers, xiv, 9, 21, 26, 29, 34, 40, 47, 111, 116, 119
equality, 16, 63–64, 70–71
equity, x, 24, 85–86, 88–89, 110
ethnicity, 25, 50, 56, 85, 123

ethnic minorities, 70, 80, 126
ethnic minority students, 56, 69
evidence, 58–59, 63–65, 74–76
evidence of progress, 63–65, 67, 70, 72
exercise, 86–87, 133, 136
expectations, 40, 51, 60–61, 71, 73, 75, 78–79, 95–96, 100–101, 109, 114
expertise, xiii–xiv, 1, 8, 11–12, 48, 88, 96, 109, 114, 116, 118

failure, xii, 11, 45, 51, 61, 138
family, 9–10, 13, 22, 25, 27, 45, 47, 56, 58–59, 61–62, 75–76, 78–79, 96–97, 100, 105
fear, 35, 46, 59, 63–67, 71, 78, 86, 89–90, 116, 124
female professors, 72, 81, 126, 131
frustrations, xi, 25, 44, 67, 70, 96, 109, 113–14

gender, 2, 6, 10, 14–15, 25, 50, 57, 59, 61, 64, 72
gendered racism, 15–16
graduate school, 11, 33, 44, 50, 56, 63, 65, 67, 73–74, 77, 79
graduate students, 11, 33, 44, 48, 65, 129
graduation, 3, 47–48, 60, 122, 128
growth, 46, 63, 87, 96, 114

hair, 19, 56, 64, 69, 99
hairstyles, 5, 69
harassment, 15, 40
harm, xiv, 72, 86, 104
HBCUs (Historically Black College or University), 20, 24, 32–33, 47, 58, 110, 134
health, mental, 88, 125
higher education, 16
high school, 32, 45, 58
Historically Black College or University. *See* HBCUs
hypervisibility, 2, 4, 7, 12

identity, xvi, 1, 4, 15, 67, 69, 102, 127

Index

identity politics, xi–xii, xvi–xvii, 15
imposter phenomenon, 79–80, 124–25, 131
imposter syndrome, x, 62–63, 130–31
inclusion, x, 3–4, 14, 16, 21, 24, 68, 85, 88–89
inclusion work, 85, 110
intersectionality, 2, 12, 15, 59, 64, 106
invisibility, 2, 4, 7, 12

joy, ix, 52, 102, 136, 138

knowledge, x, 1, 32, 50, 58, 61–63, 71, 74–75, 91

leadership, 49, 83, 101, 112, 114, 117, 137
learning, x, xvi, 10, 18, 53, 59, 87, 89, 131, 138
life, 18, 20–21, 47, 61, 63–66, 77, 84, 88, 98, 101, 104, 106, 122–24
love, 27–28, 33, 88, 104, 106
luck, 46–50, 53
lucky, 43, 46, 52, 77, 97
luxury, 57–58, 60, 74

mental health, 88, 125
mentees, x, 46, 50–52, 128, 130, 136
mentoring, x, 3, 5, 43–44, 46–47, 51–53, 124, 128–30, 133, 136–37
mentoring process, 20, 51
mentoring relationships, 46, 52, 131
mentors, x–xi, 12–13, 20–21, 27, 44–46, 50–52, 76, 79, 127–28, 130–31, 136
microaggressions, racial, 57, 81
minoritized communities, 92, 115

name, 18, 20–21, 25, 27, 68, 72–73, 76, 81, 110, 112, 126, 131, 135
network, ix, 46, 50, 104, 117
novice, 62–63, 75

opportunities, x, xv, 5, 9, 23, 46, 51–52, 59–62, 85, 110, 112

organizations, xiv, 4, 34, 63, 110, 113–15, 117–18, 137–38
outsiders, 5–6, 135

pandemic, 25, 28, 83, 90, 97, 134
parents, 13, 19, 31, 33, 45, 47, 64, 70, 86, 97, 123, 127
paths, 27, 47, 60–61, 76–77, 128, 130
peace, ix, xvi, 20, 25–26, 88
peers, 6, 10, 56–57, 70, 73
power, ix, 4, 12–14, 23, 27, 45, 85, 96, 113–14, 126–27, 137
power structure, 10, 46, 114
Predominantly White Institutions. *See* PWI
presentation, 62, 69, 84, 86–87, 89, 133
president, xii, 122
privilege, 4, 64–66, 70, 81, 91, 105, 122, 127
professional spaces, xi, 6, 22
professional titles, 66, 72
professional women, 12–13, 61
professors, 43, 48–49, 72, 74, 80, 126, 131; female, 72, 81, 126, 131
programs, 31, 39, 45, 47–49, 56, 61, 63, 65
progress, 55, 63–65, 67, 70, 72, 91, 103, 115, 137
psychologists, 44, 122
psychology, 24, 44, 47, 60–61, 70, 77, 85, 121, 131
PWI (Predominantly White Institutions), 13, 67, 69, 74, 119, 129

race, xiii, xv, 2–3, 6, 14–16, 19, 25, 32, 57–59, 70, 74, 80, 85
racism, x, xii, 2–3, 8–9, 12, 15, 19, 26, 33–35, 100, 102, 134; systemic, 19, 31, 90; unintentional, 93, 107
racist, 14, 28–29, 32, 87
racist treatment, 29, 106
reflection, 7, 55, 62, 71, 76, 85, 99, 123
relationships, 3, 5, 30, 32, 38, 50–52, 67, 69, 76–77, 128, 130, 135
replacements, 28, 43–53, 131

resources, x, xv, 3, 45, 70, 75, 97–98, 104–5, 113, 136
responsibility, ix, 9, 12–13, 58, 71, 97, 118
résumé whitening, 68
retreats, 98–99, 102, 104
risk, 2, 8–9, 33, 59, 68, 79, 104, 138
role model, 23, 43, 74, 124, 127–28, 131
roles, 2, 6, 11, 15, 18, 21–22, 68, 72, 109, 114, 116, 118–19, 129–30
rules, xiii, 58–59, 97, 123–25

sacrifices, 77–78, 83
safety, 64–67, 69, 71–72, 89, 98, 105
scholarly work, 68, 75
scholars, 26, 51, 61, 73, 89
school, 10, 18–20, 31–32, 34–35, 37, 39–40, 44, 47–48, 56, 61, 67, 74, 124
self-care, 13, 27, 102–3, 106, 117
semester, 19, 24, 35, 47, 50, 60, 71, 73, 117
services, xiii, 8, 60, 65, 68, 87, 104, 112
shame, 25, 122, 127
social work degree, 85
society, xiii, 32, 55, 57, 59, 63, 70–71, 102
spaces; brown, 58, 66; safe, 13
stereotypes, 55, 57, 59–60, 103
stereotype threat, 59, 62–63, 81
strength, 8, 12–13, 18, 62, 77, 79, 95, 100, 114
stress, 28, 40, 78, 97, 101, 105, 127, 134
Strong Black Woman, 7–8, 15, 55, 78–79
success, xii–xiii, xv–xvi, 13, 45, 49, 58–61, 77–79, 122, 128, 131, 135
supervisor, xiv, xvi, 35, 38–39

support, xiii, xv, 10, 13, 21–23, 25, 27, 51–52, 76–77, 95–97, 103, 105–6, 117, 129, 137
systemic racism, 19, 31, 90
systems, x, xiii–xv, 1, 5, 10, 88, 91, 95, 113, 118, 124–25, 135

teach, 23, 48, 70–72, 74, 77, 122, 127, 130
teachers, 10, 18–19, 32, 35, 39, 43, 56–57, 92
teaching, 70, 73, 85, 91
threat, 10, 15, 32, 65
trainings, 19–20, 24, 38, 86, 88, 90, 112, 118, 122

uncomfortable conversations, xvi, 87, 103
United States, 15, 63–64, 66, 84, 88, 95, 100, 103–4, 134

voices, ix–x, xii, xiv, xvi, 7, 12, 24, 31, 103–4, 125, 128

White colleagues, xvi, 129
Whiteness, 31, 34, 135
White privilege, 64, 68, 80
White spaces, 31, 56, 58, 62, 65–66, 76, 113, 119
White students, 56, 60, 66, 74
White supremacy, xi, 32, 41, 102
White woman, 8, 11, 35, 125
White women, 1, 32, 34, 37, 67, 103, 125
work environment, 3, 5, 11, 36, 116
workforce, 1–4, 7, 9, 13, 109
work-life balance, 74, 76
workplaces, inclusive, 14

young Black woman, 17–18, 23, 50, 135

About the Contributors

EDITORS

Dr. Sharon L. Bowman (PhD, HSPP, ABPP, LMHC) is professor and chair in the Department of Counseling Psychology, Social Psychology, and Counseling at Ball State University in Muncie, Indiana. She also has a private practice in the community. Her doctoral degree is in counseling psychology from Southern Illinois University-Carbondale; she completed her internship at the University of Delaware's counseling center. Dr. Bowman has been department chair for thirty-two years; she was doctoral program director for three years. Dr. Bowman is a fellow of the American Psychological Association through Divisions 17 (Society of Counseling Psychology) and 45 (Society for the Psychological Study of Culture, Ethnicity, and Race). She was the 2014 president of Division 17, Society of Counseling Psychology. Dr. Bowman was a member of the Indiana State Psychology Board (licensure board) for twenty years. She is board certified in counseling psychology; she is the past president of the American Board of Counseling Psychology, and also the counseling representative to the ABPP Board of Trustees. Dr. Bowman currently serves on the Indiana Behavioral Health Commission, mandated to examine mental health needs and solutions for the residents of Indiana. She is also a longtime disaster mental health volunteer and instructor for the American Red Cross, working in local, regional, and national capacities. Dr. Bowman's research and clinical interests are in supervision, mentoring, and training domestic and international students, disaster psychology, and broadly defined issues of diversity.

Dr. Rosalyn D. Davis (PhD, HSPP) is licensed psychologist and clinical associate professor of psychology at Indiana University Kokomo. She completed her undergraduate degree in psychology at Fisk University, master's degree in counseling at University of Texas at San Antonio, and doctoral degree in counseling psychology at Ball State University where she connected with Dr. Bowman. She teaches undergraduate and graduate courses across the curriculum but with a special focus to infuse issues of diversity, equity, and inclusion throughout her courses. She has served as the inaugural faculty diversity liaison for academic affairs to assist her colleagues and institution to ensure students have been exposed to DEI-related issues specific to each discipline. She serves as a mentor to several current and former students who primarily from historically excluded backgrounds. She also lectures at community agencies and other academic institutions with a focus on mental health and diversity, equity, and inclusion. Her research focuses on mentoring, relationships, and supporting historically excluded students in higher education settings. She serves on the editorial board of the Counseling Psychologist, the Midwestern Psychological Association Council, and the Society for the Future of Higher Education.

CONTRIBUTORS

Dr. Vanessa Costello-Harris (PhD) is originally from Southern California and completed her BA in psychology at California State University-Fullerton. She completed her MA and PhD in psychology at Miami University, Ohio. Dr. Costello-Harris spent five years as an assistant professor of psychology at Indiana University-Kokomo and researched topics surrounding necessary supports for college students with disabilities and promoting inclusive teaching practices. In 2019, she decided to transition from teaching within an academic setting and complete the requirements to become a board-certified behavior analyst. She now works within an applied clinical setting, working with children and teens diagnosed with autism.

Rana Dotson is entrepreneurial promoter of social and economic inclusion. She is a fourth-generation daughter of Black Church pioneers. Rana has worked for more than twenty years on human rights, public policy, and economic and international development. She is a senior international affairs officer at the Bureau of International Labor Affairs (ILAB), the US Department of Labor's international arm working to fight labor exploitation around the world. Her most recent project, COGICgarden, is an initiative promoting economic and food security in partnership with the Black Church Food Security Network. She is a co-founder and lead organizer for Border of Lights. Rana holds an MPP from the Maryland School of Public Policy and BA in political science from Tuskegee University. She is a fellow with the International Career Advancement Program (ICAP), and National Security

Education Program (NSEP) David L. Boren Graduate Fellowship. She lives in the DC metro area with her family.

Shantel Gaillard holds a master's of clinical mental health degree from Ball State University where she is a doctoral student in counseling psychology. She is the president of the Black Graduate Student Association at Ball State University. Shantel gained unique insights into racial dynamics affecting Black women's often unacknowledged labor when she matriculated through a historically Black university and then multiple predominantly white universities. Shantel's experiences as a Black female public health professional have given her a unique vantage point to see a particular set of gaps. She has dedicated her career to helping mend them throughout her academic journey and in future professional practice.

Kimberly Morris (PhD, HSPP) is a licensed clinical psychologist who completed her training at Indiana University-Bloomington. She has more than twenty years of professional experience as a clinician and teacher. She works in an outpatient setting and treats adults who have symptoms of a mood disorder and/or trauma symptoms using evidence-based treatments. She is passionate about helping people live their best lives.

Jovan Shumpert is a human, woman, daughter, mother, sister, therapist, and womanist. She is a native of St. Louis, Missouri. Jovan received both a BA in psychology and MS in clinical mental health counseling from North Carolina Agricultural and Technical State University, a Historically Black College/University (HBCU). Jovan currently works as a counselor in counseling services at her alma mater. She is also the owner of Becoming.Growing.Learning. LLC, a private practice where she specializes in working with folx in early adulthood, women's issues, racism, and those having challenges with anxiety and depression. Jovan is LGBTQIA+ affirming. She has a special interest in Black women and how their intersectional identities impact their lives and mental health.

www.ingramcontent.com/pod-product-compliance
Lightning Source LLC
Chambersburg PA
CBHW020125010526
44115CB00008B/973